Student Workbook

for

Psyk.trek™ *2.0*
A Multimedia Introduction to Psychology

Andrew Peck
Pennsylvania State University

THOMSON

WADSWORTH

Australia • Canada • Mexico • Singapore • Spain • United Kingdom • United States

Printed in The United States of America
3 4 5 6 7 07 06 05 04

Printer: Phoenix Color Corp

ISBN: 0-534-63796-5

For more information about our products,
contact us at:
Thomson Learning Academic Resource Center
1-800-423-0563

For permission to use material from this text,
contact us by:
Phone: 1-800-730-2214
Fax: 1-800-731-2215
Web: http://www.thomsonrights.com

For more information contact:
Wadsworth-Thomson Learning
10 Davis Drive
Belmont, CA 94002-3098
USA

Asia
Thomson Learning
5 Shenton Way #01-01
UIC Building
Singapore 068808

Australia/ New Zealand
Thomson Learning
102 Dodds Street
South Street
Southbank, Victoria 3006
Australia

Canada
Nelson
1120 Birchmount Road
Toronto, Ontario M1K 5G4
Canada

Europe/Middle East/South Africa
Thomson Learning
High Holborn House
50/51 Bedford Row
London WC1R 4LR
United Kingdom

Latin America
Thomson Learning
Seneca, 53
Colonia Polanco
11560 Mexico D.F.
Mexico

Spain/ Portugal
Paraninfo
Calle/Magallanes, 25
28015 Madrid, Spain

Contents

1 WHAT IS 'PSYK.TREK'?

Psyk.trek 2.0 is a multimedia CD-ROM intended to introduce students to the science of psychology. It is designed as a supplement to Wayne Weiten's introductory text, *Psychology: Themes & Variations, 6e* (Weiten, 2004), or other introductory books. It is not meant to expand the content of the introductory course, but rather to enhance students' *understanding* of much of the content usually covered in introductory psychology.

In designing *Psyk.trek,* Wayne Weiten set out to create dynamic, new, interactive pathways to learning about psychology. Among other things, he hoped to achieve the following goals.

1. Promote more active learning. In the last decade, one of the most influential "movements" in psychology has been that advocating active learning (Mathie et al., 1993). Most professors are constantly looking for new ways to incorporate active learning into their classrooms. But it is not easy to come up with good active learning exercises and they take up a great deal of precious classroom time. *Psyk.trek* provides students with many new opportunities for active learning, with relatively little effort on the professor's part, and minimal loss of class time, because students can complete activities and exercises on their own.

2. Reach out to visual learners. Students have varied learning styles and not everyone learns best from text. Over the years, Weiten has had a great many students who diligently and carefully studied their textbooks, but still had great difficulty mastering the concepts and ideas covered in those books. In contrast to a traditional textbook, *Psyk.trek* provides a much more visual approach to learning key concepts. Some of the students who don't handle text well are likely to blossom in *Psyk.trek's* visual learning environment. Moreover, even students who do work effectively with text will benefit as they get a second viable pathway for learning the same material. Research in cognitive psychology suggests that encoding information both semantically and visually can result in enhanced understanding and memory (Paivio, 1986).

3. Enhance computer literacy. Today's students must acquire computer skills. Moreover, there is some preliminary evidence that computer-assisted instruction can enhance students' learning (Baker, Hale, & Gifford, 1997; Forsyth & Archer, 1997). Cognizant of these realities, psychology faculty have been keenly interested in incorporating computers into their classes more effectively. But they have been largely thwarted by a lack of comprehensive, quality programs to work with. Hopefully, *Psyk.trek* will provide psychology teachers with a software tool that will meet their students' needs.

> Visit us on the Web for up-to-the-minute online explorations and exceptional study tools!!
> http://psychology.wadsworth.com/

2 GETTING STARTED

System Requirements

Psyk.trek 2.0 is a hybrid CD-ROM that will run on both the Windows and Macintosh platforms. The system requirements listed below are baseline specifications—that is, the minimum level systems that can be expected to run the software in an adequate manner. *Psyk.trek 2.0* is not designed to run optimally on these systems. The application will perform commensurate to the capabilities of higher-powered systems. *Psyk.trek 2.0* is a stand-alone application intended for use by individual students. The program does not support use by multiple users over a network.

Macintosh System Requirements
- System 8.5 or later
- 32 MB RAM, 640 x 480 Display
- 8x CD-ROM, 16 bit sound card
- QuickTime 5.0 (included on CD)

PC/Windows System Requirements
- Windows 95, 98, ME, or XP
- 200 MHz Pentium
- 32 MB RAM, 640 x 480 Display
- 8x CD-ROM, 16 bit sound card
- QuickTime 5.0 (included on CD)

Technical Assistance
If you have any questions please contact a Wadsworth technology representative

Phone: 800-423-0563
Email: support@kdc.com
Fax: 859-647-5045

Installation Information

Psyk.trek 2.0 itself does not require any installation procedure and does not require any space on the user's hard drive! This approach offers a variety of advantages as students do not have to worry about whether they have adequate space on their hard drive, they do not have to be concerned about an installation procedure changing settings in their system, and they do not have to uninstall anything when they finish their course.

For optimal results in playing *Psyk.trek 2.0* videos, you'll need to use QuickTime 5.0. If you do not currently have version 5.0 loaded on your computer, you can install it directly from the CD by opening the QT folder, double-clicking on the install program (QT.exe for Windows, QuickTime Installer for Mac) and following the installation directions onscreen.

Launching *Psyk.trek 2.0*

When you insert the *Psyk.trek 2.0* disk in your CD-ROM drive, the program should launch automatically (unless your autostart option has been disabled). After you quit the application, the CD can remain in your CD-ROM drive without automatically restarting. When you want to restart the program you can do so by opening and closing your CD-ROM drive.

If you are using Windows, you can also launch the application by double-clicking on the icon for your CD-ROM drive in the MY COMPUTER window, or using EXPLORER, you can double-click the file named FOR_PC.EXE on the CD.

If you are using a Macintosh, you can also launch the application by double-clicking the file named FOR_MAC.EXE on the CD (note: the file will be easier to find if you use the Mac's Icon view).

Please note: You do not have to watch the entire opening sequence every time you start the program. After the Macromedia and QuickTime logos have faded away, you can skip the remainder of the opening sequence by clicking the mouse button or pressing the Enter (or Return) key on your keyboard.

GUIDED TOUR

The Guided Tour is a narrated overview of how *Psyk.trek* works. You can enter the Guided Tour from *Psyk.trek's* opening screen *by clicking the picture of Pavlov and his staff that hangs in the sky on the right*. You can also enter the Guided Tour from most locations in the Interactive Learning Modules, the Interactive Study Guide, or the Simulations by clicking Guided Tour (see ❶ in Figure 2.1) on the Preferences submenu that is accessed by clicking the ψ❷ on the navigation cross.

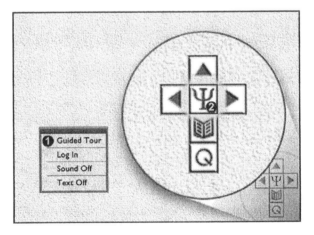

Figure 2.1. Accessing the Guided Tour from the navigation cross.

You can go to specific parts of the Guided Tour by clicking the outline entries (see ❶ in Figure 2.2) listed on the first screen of the Guided Tour. The EXIT option ❷ takes you back to your previous location before you entered the Guided Tour. It can return you to specific locations in the Interactive Learning Modules, the Interactive Study Guide, or the Simulations. Or it can return you to *Psyk.trek's* opening screen, if you accessed the Guided Tour from there.

The red buttons in the upper right corner are used for navigation within the Guided Tour. The red backward button ❸ moves you backward one screen, so you can go over a topic a second time. Within the Guided Tour, the red up button ❹ returns you to the opening screen of the Guided Tour. If you are at the opening screen of the Guided Tour, the up button takes you back to your previous location before you entered the Guided Tour. The red forward button ❺ moves you forward one screen. If it flashes, the program is waiting for you to click it to move forward, when you are ready.

Figure 2.2. The opening screen of the Guided Tour.

3 GENERAL NAVIGATION

Psyk.trek consists of four main components: the Interactive Learning Modules, the Video Selector, the Simulations, and the Multimedia Glossary. These components are accessed from the opening screen, which is shown in Figure 5.1. The user navigates among these components by manipulating the mysterious-looking cube ❶ that hovers above the surrealistic landscape. You can rotate the navigation cube to the right or left by clicking the directional arrows ❷, which appear when you roll the cursor over the area where the arrows are shown. Clicking the face of the navigation cube takes you to the component shown.

Figure 3.1. The opening screen of *Psyk.trek*.

Psyk.trek's ancillary components—the Guided Tour, Web Links, and Credits—can also be accessed from the opening screen, by clicking the three photos hanging in the sky (see Figure 3.1). Clicking the photo of the infant on the visual cliff ❸ takes you to the Credits component of *Psyk.trek*. If you click the photo of the Rubin vase ❹, you will go to the Web Links component of *Psyk.trek*. Clicking the photo of Ivan Pavlov and his staff ❺ takes you to the Guided Tour.

Clicking the ψ in the lower-right corner of the opening screen (see ❻ in Figure 3.1) brings up the submenu shown in Figure 3.2 (see next page). Clicking the X ❶ in the CLOSE bar closes the menu. Clicking GUIDED TOUR ❷ takes you to the Main menu of the Guided Tour. Clicking CREDITS ❸ takes you to the Credits component of *Psyk.trek*. Clicking QUIT ❹ allows you to quit the application and exit *Psyk.trek*.

Figure 3.2. Opening screen with submenu displayed.

Once you are in the various components of *Psyk.trek*, you move about by using the navigation buttons found in the lower-right corner of each screen (see Figure 3.3). Clicking ψ ❶ opens the Preferences submenu. In the Preferences submenu, clicking GUIDED TOUR ❷ takes you to the Main menu of the Guided Tour. Students can click LOG IN ❸ to enter their name so it will appear on printed documents, such as Quiz results in the Interactive Learning Modules or Self-Test results in the Interactive Study Guide. Clicking SOUND ON/OFF ❹ toggles the sound on or off, including the narration. As a general rule, students will want the sound on, but they may occasionally need to turn the sound off if they are working in a lab or library where quiet is required. Clicking TEXT ON/OFF ❹ toggles the text of the narration on or off. The default setting is off. **If you turn this option on you can read along with the narration. This will make it much easier to complete the workbook.** Clicking the close button ❻ in the upper left corner of the Preferences submenu closes the Preferences submenu.

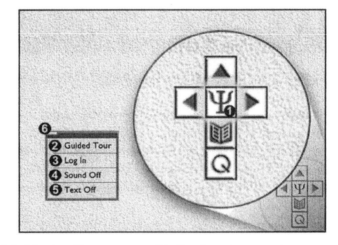

Figure 3.3. Navigation cross with Preferences submenu displayed.

The basic navigation buttons work as follows (see Figure 3.4). The up button ❶ takes you up one level in *Psyk.trek's* organizational hierarchy. If you are working in an Interactive Learning Module or a chapter of the Interactive Study Guide, this button returns you to the title screen for that module or chapter. If you are at a title screen, the up button returns you to the Selector menu for the component you are working in. The forward button ❷ moves you forward one screen. If this button flashes, the program is waiting for you to click it to move forward, when you are ready. The backward button ❸ moves you backward one screen, so you can go over a topic again. The glossary button ❹ launches the Multimedia Glossary. The quit button ❺ allows you to quit the application and exit *Psyk.trek.*

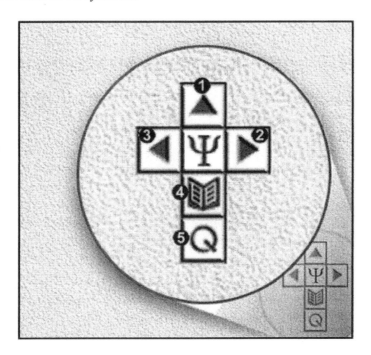

Figure 3.4. The navigation cross.

4 INTERACTIVE LEARNING MODULES

The main component of *Psyk.trek* consists of the 62 Interactive Learning Modules that present thousands of graphics, hundreds of ground-breaking animations, hundreds of photos, approximately four hours of narration, over 35 carefully-selected videos, and about 150 uniquely visual concept checks and quizzes that should enable students to achieve new levels of understanding of much of the basic content of introductory psychology.

The Interactive Learning Modules are organized into the 12 topical units listed on the left side of the Selector menu shown in Figure 4.1. You can click the items in this list❶ to select specific

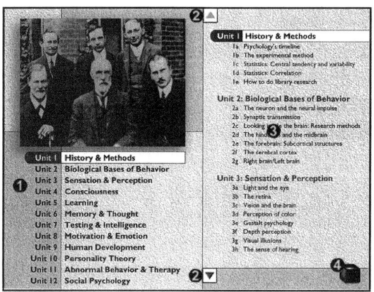

Figure 4.1. The Selector menu for the Interactive Learning Modules.

units. You can also click the scroll buttons❷ to move through the list of Interactive Learning Modules. Clicking a specific topic in the list of modules❸ takes you to the beginning of that module. If you click the small rotating cube in the lower right corner❹, you will be returned to the opening screen and the navigation cube.

Each module begins with a title screen (see Figure 4.2 on the next page) that provides an outline❶ of the module's contents. Each module ends with a Review and a Quiz❷. You can go directly to a specific part of a module by clicking that entry in the outline. Each title screen also includes a button that will take you to related web links❸. If there is a Simulation relevant to a module, the title screen includes a button that will take you to the Simulation❹. To begin proceeding through the module, just click the forward button❺. Clicking the up button❻ on the title screen takes you back to the Selector menu for the Interactive Learning Modules.

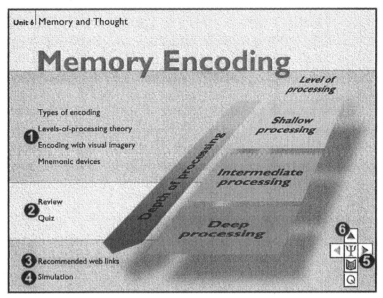

Figure 4.2. A title screen from an Interactive Learning Module.

Important--- Important--- Important
Sometimes rapidly clicking the forward or backward buttons repeatedly causes the narrations to get out of synch with the visual material shown onscreen. In stead of 'scrolling' through Module screens, use the outline entries on the opening screen to jump to the section you desire. If narrations get out of synch with visual material you must return to the opening screen of the module (in effect, restarting the module) to fix the problem. You can then use the outline entries to return to the section you were in when you encountered difficulties.

Each module is fully narrated, so students can focus their attention on the charts, diagrams, figures, and animations that unfold onscreen. However, users may choose to have the text of the narration appear onscreen (see❶ in Figure 4.3 on the next page) so that they can take as much time as they like to review what was said. The narration text can be turned on or off by accessing the Preferences submenu❷. **Turning narration text on will make it much easier to complete the workbook.**

When glossary terms are first introduced in the text of the narration, they are shown in blue boldface type (see ❸ Figure 4.3). If you click a blue glossary term, its definition will appear in a small box superimposed on the screen❹. The definition disappears when you click the close button in the top left corner of the definition box❺.

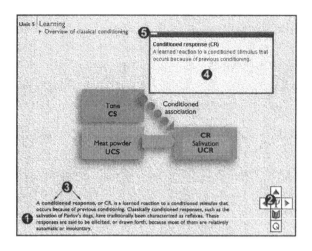

Figure 4.3. A screen from an Interactive Learning Module, with a definition displayed.

Throughout each Interactive Learning Module, a header in the upper left corner indicates your current location (see ❶ in Figure 4.4). It shows the specific unit and module that you are working in. If there is a video segment relevant to the content of a specific screen, a video icon will migrate onscreen. If you roll the cursor over the video icon, you will see a short description of the video❷. Clicking the video icon brings up the video, which you can view by clicking the play button. The videos are very brief clips (generally less than a minute) that provide illustrative material that is closely related to the contents of the modules.

As students move through the Interactive Learning Modules, they will often be asked to click specific parts of diagrams or drawings to learn more about them. The clickable portions of diagrams or drawings will generally light up in yellow when the cursor is rolled over them. In some cases, students will be asked to click text that appears on screen (see ❸ in Figure 4.4). Clickable text is always shown in blue and lights up in yellow when the cursor is rolled over it.

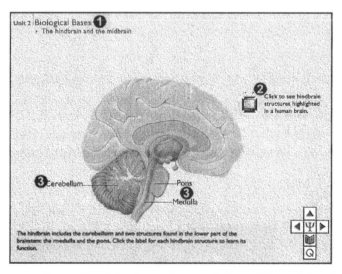

Figure 4.4. A screen from the interior of a module, with a video icon displayed.

Most modules include one or more Concept Checks that permit students to check their understanding of the material just covered (see Figure 4.5). Concept Check questions are answered by clicking the choices onscreen. Users get immediate feedback about whether their answers are correct or incorrect (the words "That's correct!" or "That's incorrect!" are flashed onscreen, accompanied by corresponding sound effects). If users answer incorrectly, they can keep trying until they choose the correct answer. Clicking the correct answer or the forward button advances the student to the next screen.

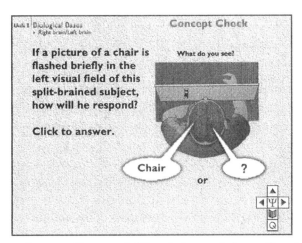

Figure 4.5. A screen from a Concept Check in an Interactive Learning Module.

Each module includes a Review section that provides a brief recap of the main ideas introduced in the module (see Figure 4.6). For the most part, the Reviews do not include animations or interactivity, but they are narrated.

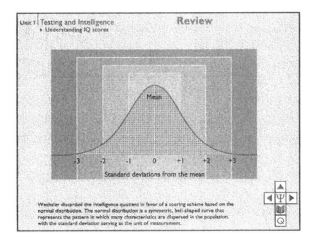

Figure 4.6. A Review screen from Module 7c.

Some Reviews end with Rollover Reviews, which permit students to systematically examine whether they have made the connections between various technical terms and the structures they refer to in crucial diagrams (see Figure 4.7 on next page). For example, in Module 2d, students can roll the cursor over the names of various brain structures ❶ to highlight those structures in a diagram of the brain❷. They can also reverse the process, rolling over various brain structures to highlight their names.

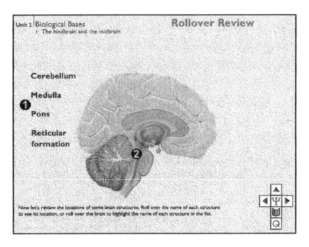

Figure 4.7. An example of a Rollover Review.

Each module ends with a Quiz (see Figure 4.8). Students answer Quiz questions by clicking choices onscreen. They get immediate feedback about whether their answers are correct or incorrect. If an answer is incorrect, they can keep trying until they choose the correct answer. However, in computing Quiz scores the program counts only their first answer to each question. Clicking the correct answer advances the Quiz to the next question. The glossary, forward, and backward buttons are disabled during a Quiz. In keeping with *Psyk.trek's* highly visual approach to teaching, whenever possible the quizzes are also highly visual in nature. In other words, the quizzes frequently require students to wrestle with complex diagrams and respond in the context of those diagrams.

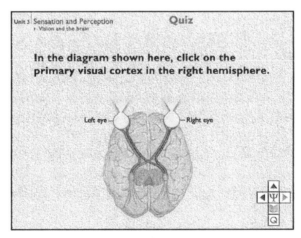

Figure 4.8. A quiz question from an Interactive Learning Module.

At the end of a Quiz, the program will report the student's score onscreen (see ❶ in Figure 4.9 on next page). Students can click the Print button ❷ onscreen to print a copy of their Quiz results, or the Email option ❸ to send a copy of their results to an instructor. Students can include their name on printed or emailed information ❹ if they have used the login option on the Preferences submenu❺ or the Remember to Log In option❻.

The print and email options were included so that professors could assign specific modules and require students to turn in some evidence that they had completed the modules in a satisfactory manner. Please bear in mind, however, that this plan depends on an "honor system." It would not be all that difficult for a student to go directly to the Quiz (without completing the module), take the Quiz while jotting down the correct answers, retake the Quiz answering everything correctly, and then print some impressive results. In light of this reality, if you choose to have students submit Quiz results, I would view these results as "homework" assignments and not weigh them heavily in the grading process. Like many homework assignments, the module quizzes could be faked or copied from a friend.

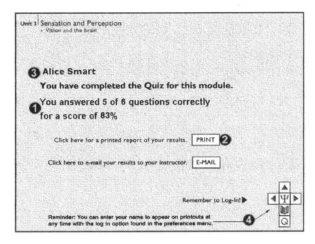

Figure 4.9. An example of Quiz feedback, which can be printed.

When students reach the final screen of a module (see Figure 4.10), they can choose to go to the next module❶; retake the Quiz❷; see a suggested list of related readings❸; or go to a Simulation❹if one is pertinent to that module.

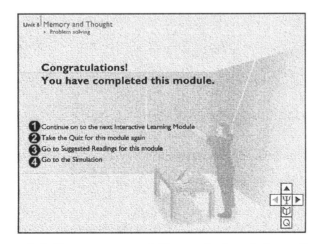

Figure 4.10. A Congratulations screen at the end of an Interactive Learning Module.

5 SIMULATIONS

Psyk.trek simulations, are highly interactive demonstrations that allow students to experience psychological phenomena first-hand and to see research methods in action. Students can access the Simulations from the Interactive Learning Modules or by clicking the Simulations face of the navigation cube on *Psyk.trek's* opening screen (see Figure 5.1).

Figure 5.1. The opening screen with the Simulations face of the navigation cube showing.

The Simulations Selector menu allows students to move among the simulations. To go to a specific simulation, the user simply clicks the title in the list (see ❶ in Figure 5.2). Clicking the small rotating cube in the bottom right corner ❷ returns the user to *Psyk.trek's* opening screen and the navigation cube.

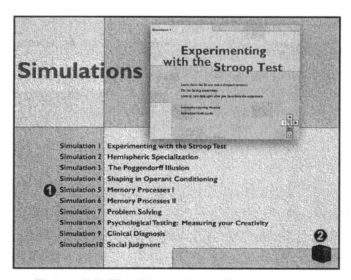

Figure 5.2. The Simulations Selector menu.

Each simulation begins with a title screen that lists the various parts of the simulation (see Figure 5.3). You can go directly to a particular part of the simulation by clicking that entry in the list❶. A button that will take the user to the Selector menu for the Interactive Learning Modules is also available❷. Students move about in the Simulations by using the navigation buttons found in the lower right corner❸.

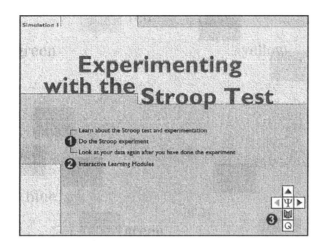

Figure 5.3. A title screen from a simulation.

The navigation buttons in the simulations generally function the same way as in other components of *Psyk.trek*. However, when a student is in the midst of a demonstration or data collection, some buttons may be temporarily disabled. As in the Interactive Learning Modules, clickable text is shown in blue (see ❶ in Figure 5.4). Most of the simulations permit students to collect data, which is often summarized in graphs (see ❷ in Figure 5.4). This process allows students to see how "real" data are converted into graphs and gives them practice in interpreting graphical displays of data. Many Simulations provide students with opportunities to analyze their own data❸. All Simulations provide opportunities for students to print out their results or to email their results to an instructor.

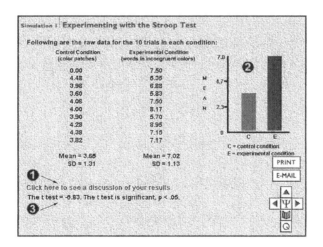

Figure 5.4. Students often collect and analyze data in *Psyk.trek* simulations.

6 STUDENT RESOURCES

Video Selector

Psyk.trek includes over 35 video clips that can be accessed from various locations (some video clips are relevant to more than one module). The Video Selector allows students to find and view the video clips contained on the *Psyk.trek* CD without searching through the Interactive Learning Modules. The Video Selector should help students who want to review *Psyk.trek* video clips as they study. Students can access the Video Selector by clicking the Video Selector face of the navigation cube on *Pysk.Trek's* opening screen (see Figure 6.1).

Figure 6.1 The opening screen with the Video Selector face of the cube showing.

Students can use the Video Selector menu (see Figure 6.2 on next page) to choose specific video clips from *Psyk.trek*. Video descriptions are listed on the left side of the menu❶. When the mouse cursor passes over a description, a blue bullet appears next to that description❷ and a still shot from the video appears on the right side of the display❸. Students and instructors can use the up and down arrows❹ to scroll through the entire list of video descriptions. Clicking on the small rotating cube in the bottom right corner❺ returns the user to *Psyk.trek's* opening screen and the navigation cube.

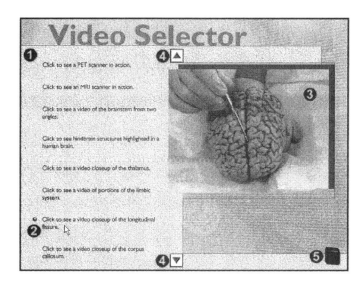

Figure 6.2. The Video Selector menu.

Clicking a description activates the corresponding video clip (see Figure 6.3). Click on the speaker button❶ to activate video volume controls. Click on the arrow button❷ to play the video. This button becomes a pause button when the video is playing. Click on the fast-forward and rewind icons❸ to control the video.

Figure 6.3. A screen from the Video Selector when a movie has been selected.

MULTIMEDIA GLOSSARY

The Multimedia Glossary allows students to look up more than 800 important psychological terms, access hundreds of pronunciations for obscure words, and pull up hundreds of related diagrams, photos, and videos that will enhance their understanding of psychology's vocabulary.

The Multimedia Glossary can be accessed from most locations in the Interactive Learning Modules or the Simulations by clicking the Glossary button found on the navigation cross. You can also enter the Multimedia Glossary from *Psyk.trek's* opening screen by clicking the appropriate face of the navigation cube (see Figure 6.4).

Figure 6.4 The opening screen with the Multimedia Glossary face of the cube showing.

Once you are in the Multimedia Glossary, you can select specific terms by clicking the items in the alphabetical list (see ❶ in Figure 6.5) and the appropriate definitions will appear in the box below❷. You can jump around in the alphabet by clicking the letters on the left ❸ or by using the scrollbar on the right❹. The forward and backward buttons move you through the list of terms one at a time❺. To search for a specific technical term, type the term in the Search window❻ and then click the adjacent Search button (or press the Enter (Return) key).

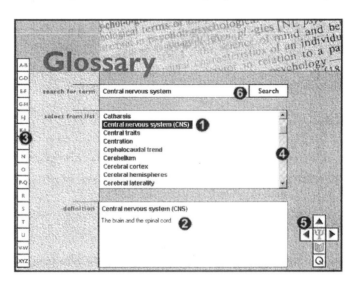

Figure 6.5. A screen from the Multimedia Glossary.

When selected, many of the terms bring up one or more of three icons that permit you to access additional information related to those terms (see Figure 6.6). If the speaker icon appears❶, you can click it to hear the pronunciation of the term. If the camera icon appears❷, you can click it to see a pertinent photo, diagram, drawing, or other type of graphic. (You can enlarge graphics by clicking on the magnifying glass icon. You can return graphics to original size by clicking on the enlarged picture.) If the video icon appears❸, you can click it to view a video clip related to the selected term.

The glossary and preferences buttons (see ❹ in Figure 6.6) are disabled when you are in the Multimedia Glossary. The up button ❺ takes you back to your previous location before you entered the Multimedia Glossary. It can return you to specific locations in the Interactive Learning Modules, the Interactive Study Guide, or the Simulations. Or it can return you to *Psyk.trek's* opening screen, if you accessed the Multimedia Glossary from there.

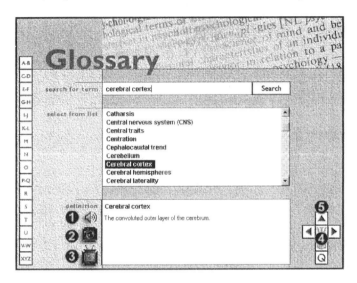

Figure 6.6. A screen from the Multimedia Glossary, with supplemental icons showing.

Web Links

The Web Links component of *Psyk.trek* provides students with a brief list of outstanding web sites that should get them launched exploring psychology on the Internet. Rather than construct a long list of web links, the concentration was on selecting sites that provide long lists of links. The recommended sites are divided into three groups: megalists, sites providing advising resources, and sites of major psychology-related organizations. You access the Web Links from *Psyk.trek's* opening screen by clicking the picture of the Rubin vase that hangs in the sky on the left (see ❶ in Figure 6.7 on the next page).

Figure 6.7. *Psyk.trek's* opening screen, with access to the Web Links highlighted.

*Psyk.*trek provides a brief description of each recommended web site, along with URLs. The URLs ❶ are "hot links" that automatically launch your web browser and take you to the destination site. Destination sites open in a separate window, allowing students to resume their *Psyk.trek* session when they are ready.

The red buttons in the lower right corner are used for navigation within the Web Links (see Figure 6.8). The red backward button ❷ moves you back one screen. Inside the Web Links, the red up button ❸ returns you to the opening screen of the Web Links component. If you are at the opening screen of the Web Links, the up button takes you back to *Psyk.trek's* opening screen and the navigation cube. The red forward button ❹ moves you forward one screen.

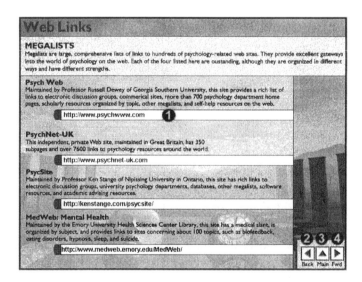

Figure 6.8. A screen from the Web Links component of *Psyk.trek*.

7 STUDENT LESSONS

Student lessons are to be used in conjunction with the interactive learning modules and simulations. Mostly, they are designed so that students do not have to re-run *Psyk.trek* whenever they want to study *Psyk.trek* information. They are also designed to:

- help students identify the important concepts in each lesson
- provide students with activities to facilitate understanding
- allow students to study *Psyk.trek* information quickly and thoroughly
- provide students with lesson outlines
- provide students with learning objectives
- provide instructors with a "paper-and-pencil" way of reviewing student learning

Students will find that lesson questions are in short answer, short essay, fill-in-the blank, and label-the-diagram formats. These formats were chosen to support a wide range of student preferences and to promote encoding and elaboration – things that benefit learning considerably (you can learn about this in Module 6b).

Students will find it much easier to complete the workbook if they turn on the narration text option by accessing the Preferences submenu (see Figure 7.1). Clicking ψ ❶ opens the Preferences submenu. In the Preferences submenu, **clicking TEXT ON/OFF ❺** toggles the text of the narration on or off. **The default setting is off.**

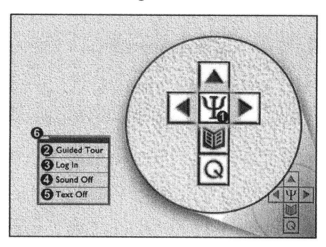

Figure 7.1. Navigation cross with Preferences submenu displayed.

NAME _____   CLASS _____

Module 1a—Psychology's timeline

Description
In this module, students learn about the people and ideas that have shaped psychology's evolution since it emerged as an independent science in the latter part of the nineteenth century.

Outline
1870-1900
1901-1950
1951-present
Review
Quiz
Recommended web links

Learning objectives
1. Summarize how Wundt, James, and Hall contributed to the early growth of psychology.
2. Summarize how Pavlov, Binet, and Washburn contributed to the early growth of psychology.
3. Summarize how Freud and Watson influenced the course of psychology's development.
4. Summarize the contributions of Terman and Wertheimer.
5. Describe the views of Rogers and Maslow.
6. Describe Skinner's views.
7. Discuss the emergence of the cognitive and physiological perspectives.
8. Describe Milgram's contribution to psychology.

Guided Learning Questions
1. Who is Wilhelm Wundt and why is his work important to Psychology?

2. Complete the thought: Structuralism asserts that the task of psychology is to .....

3. What is Functionalism? How are Functionalism and Structuralism different?

Guided Learning Questions (continued)

4. Who founded the American Psychological Association (APA)?

5. Who is Ivan Pavlov and why is his work important to Psychology?

6. Who is Alfred Binet and why is his work important to Psychology?

7. Who is Margaret Floy Washburn and why is her work important to Psychology?

8. What is Freud's thesis?

9. According to John B. Watson, why are mental processes unsuitable for study?

10. How did World War I affect the growth of Psychology?

Guided Learning Questions (continued)

11. Who is Max Wertheimer and why is he important to Psychology?

12. In the 1930's Freud's ideas contributed to the development of Psychology. How?

13. What role did World War II (and its aftermath) play in the development of Psychology?

14. What does the Humanistic School of Thought (Humanism) emphasize?

15. Briefly, what were B.F. Skinners beliefs?

16. What happened in 1956?

17. Why was Stanley Milgram's research so important?

18. What did B.F. Skinner's think about free will?

19. How did the cognitive and physiological perspectives gain prominence in the 1970s and 1980s?

NAME _____ CLASS _____

Module 1b—The experimental method

Description
In this module, students learn how psychologists conduct experiments to test their hypotheses.

Outline
Independent and dependent variables
Experimental and control groups
Examples of experiments
Variations in experiments
Review
Quiz
Recommended web links
Simulation – Experimenting with the Stroop test

Learning objectives
1. Distinguish between independent and dependent variables.
2. Distinguish between experimental and control groups.
3. Explain the logic of the experimental method.
4. Discuss the use of multiple independent or dependent variables in an experiment.

Guided Learning Questions
1. What is an experiment?

2. What is the purpose of an experiment?

3. What is an independent variable?

Guided Learning Questions (continued)

4. What is a dependent variable?

5. What is a good short cut for sorting out the independent and dependent variables in an experiment?

6. Complete the figure below:

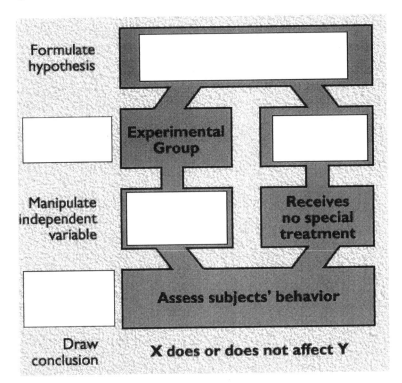

7. Finish the thought: "The Experimental Group consists of ...."

Guided Learning Questions (continued)
8. Finish the thought: "The Control Group consists of …."

9. What is Schachter's hypothesis?

10. What is the independent variable in Schachter's study?

11. How did the experimenter manipulate the independent variable (anxiety level)?

12. What is the dependent variable in Schachter's study?

13. What did Schachter find?

Guided Learning Questions (continued)

14. Did the result support the hypothesis? Explain.

15. What is Kelley's hypothesis?

16. What is the independent variable in Kelley's study?

17. How did the experimenter manipulate the independent variable?

18. What is the dependent variable in Kelley's study?

19. What did Kelley find?

Guided Learning Questions (continued)
20. Did the result support the hypothesis? Explain.

21. Why is it crucial that the experimental and control groups are similar?

22. Why would you want to study the effects of 2 independent variables at the same time?

23. Why would you want to study the effects of 2 or more dependent variables at the same time?

NAME _____   CLASS _____

Module 1c—Statistics: Central tendency and variability

Description
In this module, students learn about basic descriptive statistics and how they are used in research.

Outline
Graphing data
Measuring central tendency
Measuring variability
Review
Quiz
Recommended web links

Learning objectives
1. Describe how frequency distributions, histograms, and frequency polygons are used to organize numerical data.
2. Distinguish between the mean, median, and mode.
3. Explain how the standard deviation indexes variability.

Guided Learning Questions
1. What is statistics?

2. What does a frequency distribution show?

3. What is a histogram?

4. What is a frequency polygon?

Guided Learning Questions (continued)

5. In a frequency polygon, what does the horizontal axis list? What does the vertical axis indicate?

6. What are descriptive statistics used for?

7. What are the three measures of central tendency?

8. What is the mean? How is it calculated?

9. What is the median?

10. What is the mode?

11. Finish the thought: "When a distribution is symmetrical…"

12. Where are most scores in a negatively skewed distribution?

Guided Learning Questions (continued)

13. Draw a negatively skewed distribution below:

14. Where are most scores in a positively skewed distribution?

15. Draw a positively skewed distribution below:

16. Finish the thought: "In skewed distributions..."

17. What does variability refer to?

18. What is a standard deviation?

Guided Learning Questions (continued)

19. Finish the thought: "When variability increases…"

20. Draw the shape of the distribution when the standard deviation is low, medium and high below.

Low   Medium   High

NAME _____   CLASS _____

Module 1d—Statistics: Correlation

Description
In this module, students learn how the relationship between two variables can be measured with a statistic called *correlation*.

Outline
Positive and negative correlations
Strength of the correlation
Correlation and prediction
Correlation and causation
Review
Quiz
Recommended web links

Learning objectives
1. Explain the difference between positive and negative correlations.
2. Describe the relationship between the size of a correlation and the strength of the association it measures.
3. Explain how the magnitude and direction of a correlation are reflected in scatter diagrams.
4. Explain how the coefficient of determination indexes the predictability provided by a correlation.
5. Discuss the suitability of drawing causal conclusions based on correlational data.

Guided Learning Questions
1. What is the correlation coefficient?

2. What does a positive correlation indicate? Give an example of two variables that are positively correlated.

3. What does a negative correlation indicate? Give an example of two variables that are negatively correlated.

Guided Learning Questions (continued)

4. What does the size of the correlation coefficient indicate?

5. Using the interactive display, what happens to the strength of the relationship as the correlation coefficient moves from 0 towards +1?

6. Using the interactive display, what happens to the strength of the relationship as the correlation coefficient moves from 0 towards -1?

7. Using the interactive display, what happens to the strength of the relationship as the correlation coefficient moves from either +1 or -1 towards 0?

8. Finish the thought: "The closer the correlation comes to either -1.00 or +1.00 ..."

9. What is a scatter diagram?

10. Finish the thought: "When a correlation is perfect....."

11. What happens to the pattern of data points as the magnitude or strength of the correlation decreases? (Hint: Do they become more clustered or more spread apart?)

Guided Learning Questions (continued)

12. Finish the thought: "As the correlation increases in strength, the ability to predict one variable based on knowledge of the other variable…"

13. How is the coefficient of determination calculated?

14. What does the coefficient of determination indicate?

15. What happens to predictability as the magnitude or strength of the coefficient of determination increases?

16. A correlation between 2 variables does not tell us how the 2 variables are related. What are the 3 possibilities?

1:

2:

3:

17. Explain why correlation does not necessarily indicate causation. Give one example.

NAME _____   CLASS _____

Module 1e—How to do library research

Description
In this module, students learn how to find technical literature in psychology.

Outline
Introduction to *Psychological Abstracts*
Searching *Psychological Abstracts*
Computerized literature searches
Review
Quiz
Recommended web links

Learning objectives
1. Describe the elements of the abstracts published in *Psychological Abstracts*.
2. Describe how to use the subject and name indexes in *Psychological Abstracts*.
3. Explain the advantages of computerized literature searches.

Guided Learning Questions
1. What is a journal?

2. What does *Psychological Abstracts* contain?

3. What information does an abstract contain?

4. What do abstracts briefly describe?

Guided Learning Questions (continued)

5. What is PsycINFO?

NAME _____   CLASS _____

Module 2a—The neuron and the neural impulse

Description
In this module, students learn about neurons and how they permit communication in the nervous system.

Outline
Divisions of the nervous system
Types of cells in the nervous system
The neuron
The neural impulse
Review
Quiz
Recommended web links

Learning objectives
1. Distinguish between the central nervous system and the peripheral nervous system.
2. Provide an overview of the peripheral nervous system, including its subdivisions.
3. Describe the main functions of the two types of nervous tissue.
4. Identify the location of various parts of the neuron and discuss their functions.
5. Describe the neural impulse and absolute refractory period.

Guided Learning Questions
1. What are the two divisions of the nervous system?

2. What does the central nervous system consist of?

Guided Learning Questions (continued)

3. What are the parts of the peripheral nervous system? Describe each.

4. What are the two major types of cells discussed?

     1:

     2:

5. What do Glia cells do?

6. What do neurons do?

7. What do interneurons do?

8. What do sensory neurons do?

9. What do motor neurons do?

Guided Learning Questions (continued)

10. Label the three main parts of the neuron below:

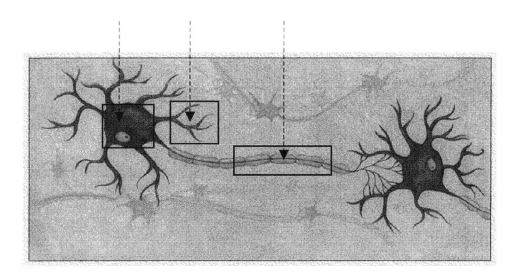

11. Describe each part of the neuron you labeled above.

    1:

    2:

    3:

12. What is myelin? What does it do?

13. What is inside a terminal button?

Guided Learning Questions (continued)

14. What are neurotransmitters?

15. What is a synapse?

16. What are the principal molecules involved in the nerve impulse? Which molecules are positively charged and which are negatively charged?

17. When is a neuron in a resting state?

18. What is resting potential?

19. What happens when a neuron is stimulated?

Guided Learning Questions (continued)

20. What is an action potential?

21. How does the action potential move along the axon?

22. What is the absolute refractory period? How long does it last?

23. Describe the "all-or-none law."

24. How do neurons convey information about the strength of a stimulus?

NAME _____   CLASS _____

Module 2b—Synaptic transmission

Description
In this module, students learn how neurons use chemical messengers to communicate at synapses.

Outline
Anatomy of the synapse
Communication at the synapse
Postsynaptic potentials
Neurotransmitters
Review
Quiz
Recommended web links

Learning objectives
1. Identify the location of key anatomical structures in the terminal button and the synapse.
2. Describe how neurons communicate at chemical synapses.
3. Describe the two types of postsynaptic potentials and how cells integrate these signals.
4. Discuss some of the functions of acetylcholine and serotonin.
5. Discuss some of the functions of dopamine and norepinephrine.
6. Discuss how GABA regulates behavior.

Guided Learning Questions
1. What is a neural impulse?

2. What is the synaptic cleft?

3. What is the presynaptic neuron?

Guided Learning Questions (continued)
4. What is the postsynaptic neuron?

5. What is inside the terminal button of the presynaptic cell?

6. What happens when an action potential arrives at an axon's terminal button?

7. What initiates a postsynaptic potential?

8. What happens to neurotransmitter molecules after producing postsynaptic potentials?

Guided Learning Questions (continued)

9. Describe the following:

Synthesis-

Release-

Binding-

Inactivation-

Reuptake-

10. Do postsynaptic potentials follow the "all-or-none law"? Explain.

11. What are the two types of messages that can be sent from cell to cell? What does each do?

Guided Learning Questions (continued)

12. Using the interactive display, what happens when you add the excitatory postsynaptic potential? What happens when you add the inhibitory postsynaptic potential?

13. What is temporal summation?

14. What is spatial summation?

15. Describe the functions of the following neurotransmitters:

Acetylcholine-

Serotonin-

Guided Learning Questions (continued)
    Dopamine-

    Norepinephrine-

    GABA-

NAME _____ CLASS _____

Module 2c—Looking inside the brain: Research methods

Description
In this module, students learn about the diverse research methods that neuroscientists use to look inside the brain.

Outline
The EEG
Lesioning
Electrical stimulation
CT scans
PET scans
MRI scans
Review
Quiz
Recommended web links

Learning objectives
1. Describe the EEG and four common brain wave patterns.
2. Describe how lesioning and ESB are used to investigate brain function.
3. Describe the new brain imaging methods that are used to study brain structure and function.

Guided Learning Questions
1. What is an EEG? What does it do?

2. Human brainwaves are usually divided into 4 principal bands. Name them.

Guided Learning Questions (continued)

3. What are Beta waves?

4. What are Alpha waves?

5. What are Theta waves?

6. What are Delta waves?

7. What is the EEG often used for?

8. How is lesioning done?

9. What is a stereotaxic instrument for?

Guided Learning Questions (continued)
10. What is ESB and what does it involve?

11. What is a CT scan?

12. What does a PET scan map?

13. Finish the thought: "Because PET scans monitor chemical processes…"

14. What is an MRI scan and what does it show?

NAME _____ CLASS _____

Module 2d—The hindbrain and the midbrain

Description
In this module, students learn how the hindbrain and midbrain contribute to the regulation of various behavioral processes.

Outline
Three major regions of the brain
The hindbrain
The midbrain
Review
Quiz
Recommended web links

Learning objectives
1. Distinguish between the hindbrain, midbrain, and forebrain.
2. Identify the location of the medulla, pons, and cerebellum, and discuss some of their functions.
3. Identify the location of the midbrain and discuss some of its functions.

Guided Learning Questions
1. The brain can be divided into 3 major regions. What are they?

1:

2:

3:

2. Which region is largest at 11 weeks? At birth?

Guided Learning Questions (continued)

3. Please complete the diagram below:

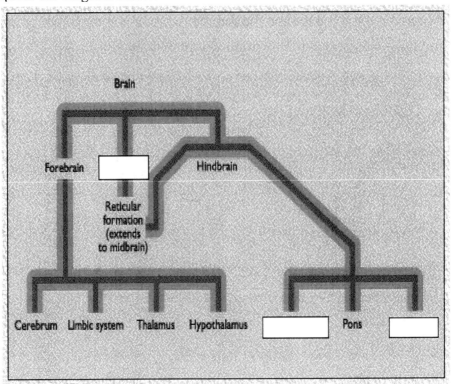

4. Please complete the diagram below:

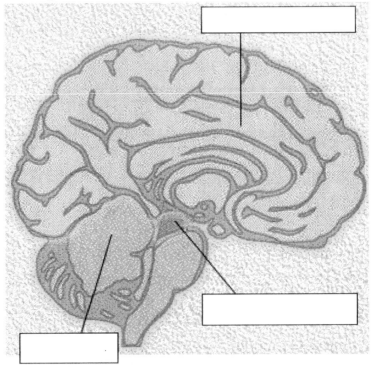

Guided Learning Questions (continued)

5. What does the hindbrain include?

6. Please complete the figure below:

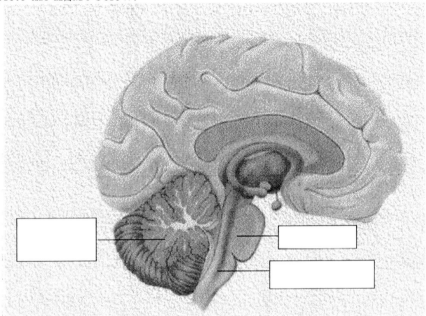

7. Why is the cerebellum important?

8. Why is the medulla important?

9. Why is the pons important?

10. What is the midbrain concerned with?

Guided Learning Questions (continued)

11. Finish the thought: "The midbrain is the origin…"

12. What does the reticular formation contribute to?

NAME _____   CLASS _____

Module 2e—The forebrain: Subcortical structures

Description
In this module, students learn about a variety of subcortical structures in the forebrain.

Outline
Thalamus
Hypothalamus
Limbic system
Review
Quiz
Recommended web links

Learning objectives
1. Identify the location of the thalamus and discuss some of its key functions.
2. Identify the location of the hypothalamus and discuss its regulation of eating behavior.
3. Discuss how the hypothalamus contributes to the regulation of the endocrine system and the autonomic nervous system.
4. Describe the nature and location of the limbic system and summarize some of its key functions.

Guided Learning Questions
1. The brain can be divided into 3 major regions. What are they? Which is the largest?

2. Please complete the diagram below:

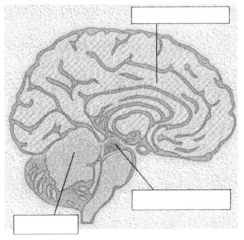

Guided Learning Questions (continued)

3. What is housed in the forebrain? Please complete the figure below?

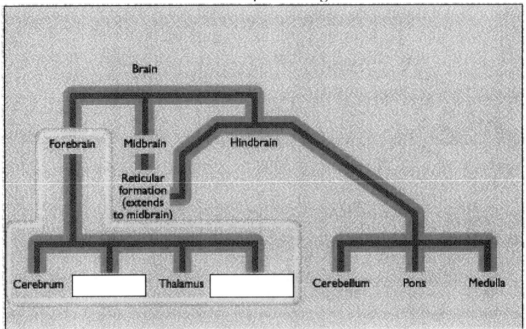

4. What are the functions of the cerebrum?

5. What is the cerebral cortex?

6. What are the functions of the thalamus?

7. Describe the many functions of the hypothalamus?

Guided Learning Questions (continued)

8. What is the endocrine system? What does it include?

9. What is the autonomic nervous system? What does it include?

10. What is the limbic system? What does it include?

11. What is the function of the hippocampus?

12. What is the function of the amygdala?

NAME _____   CLASS _____

Module 2f—The cerebral cortex

Description
In this module, students see how each cerebral hemisphere is divided into four lobes that have special functions.

Outline
Overview of the cortex
The four lobes of the cortex
Review
Quiz
Recommended web links

Learning objectives
1. Identify the location of the corpus callosum and the cerebral hemispheres.
2. Identify the location of the frontal lobe and discuss some of its functions.
3. Identify the location of the parietal lobe and discuss some of its functions.
4. Identify the location of the temporal lobe and discuss some of its functions.
5. Identify the location of the occipital lobe and discuss some of its functions.

Guided Learning Questions
1. What is the largest part of the human brain?

2. What is the longitudinal fissure?

3. What is the corpus callosum? What does it do?

4. What is gray matter?

Guided Learning Questions (continued)

5. Each brain hemisphere contains 4 lobes. What are they? Please complete the figure below:

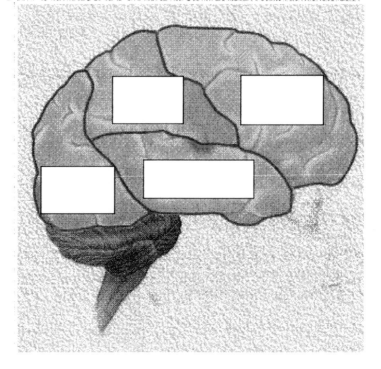

6. What is the function of the frontal lobe?

7. What is the primary motor cortex? Where is it located?

8. Finish the thought: "More of the motor cortex is devoted to...."

9. Which animal has the largest prefrontal lobe – cat, dog, chimp, or human? Which has the smallest?

Guided Learning Questions (continued)
10. What is the function of the parietal lobe?

11. What is the primary somatosensory cortex? Where is it located?

12. What is the function of the temporal lobe?

13. What is the primary auditory cortex? Where is it located?

14. What is the function of the occipital lobe?

15. What is the primary visual cortex? Where is it located?

16. Please identify the regions below:

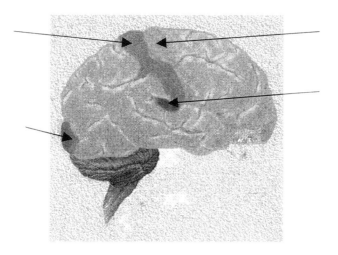

NAME _____   CLASS _____

Module 2g—Right brain/Left brain

Description
In this module, the widely publicized research on the special abilities of the right and left halves of the brain is discussed.

Outline
Overview of cerebral organization
Split-brain research
Research on perceptual asymmetries
Review
Quiz
Recommended web links
Simulation – Hemispheric Specialization

Learning objectives
1. Summarize evidence that initially led scientists to view the left hemisphere as the dominant hemisphere.
2. Describe how each hemisphere's sensory and motor connections are largely to the opposite side of the body.
3. Describe Sperry's split-brain research and its implications for hemispheric organization.
4. Describe Kimura's research on cerebral specialization in normal subjects and what this research has revealed.

Guided Learning Questions
1. What is the corpus callosum?

2. What is cerebral lateralization?

3. Where are Broca's and Wernicke's areas located? What is the function of Broca's area? What is the function of Wernicke's area?

4. Finish the thought: "Each hemisphere's primary sensory and motor connections….."

5. Finish the thought: "Visual stimuli in the left half of the visual field….."

6. Who is Roger Sperry and what did he do?

7. What happens when an image of a spoon is flashed in the left visual field of a split-brain subject?

Guided Learning Questions (continued)

8. What if the image is flashed in the right visual field?

9. What happens when an object is placed in the left hand of a split-brain subject?

10. What if the object is placed in the right hand?

11. Based on split-brain research, what does the left hemisphere usually handle? What does the right hemisphere usually handle?

12. What did Doreen Kimura do? What did she find for each of the four tasks?

NAME _____   CLASS _____

Module 3a—Light and the eye

Description
In this module, students learn about the characteristics of light and the structure and functioning of the eye.

Outline
The characteristics of light
Determinants of hue, brightness, and saturation
The structure of the eye
Accommodation
Nearsightedness and farsightedness
Review
Quiz
Recommended web links

Learning objectives
1. List the three properties of light and the aspects of visual perception that they influence.
2. Identify the location of the lens, pupil, cornea, iris, and retina and discuss their functions.
3. Explain the process of accommodation in vision.
4. Distinguish between nearsightedness and farsightedness.

Guided Learning Questions

1. What is light?

Guided Learning Questions (continued)

2. Label the figure:

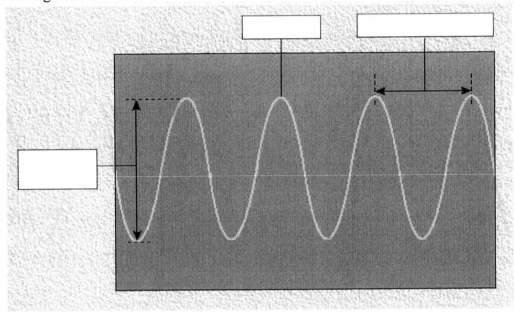

3. Draw pictures of waves with the following characteristics:

Wavelength

	Short	Long
Low		
High		

Amplitude

4. Finish the thought: "Fewer wavelengths ....."

5. Wavelength is the principal determinant of _____.

6. Amplitude is the main factor of _____.

7. Saturation is largely a function of _____.

Guided Learning Questions (continued)

8. What kind of wavelengths can insects see? What kind of wavelengths can many fish and reptiles see?

9. What is the retina?

10. What is the cornea?

11. Label the figure below:

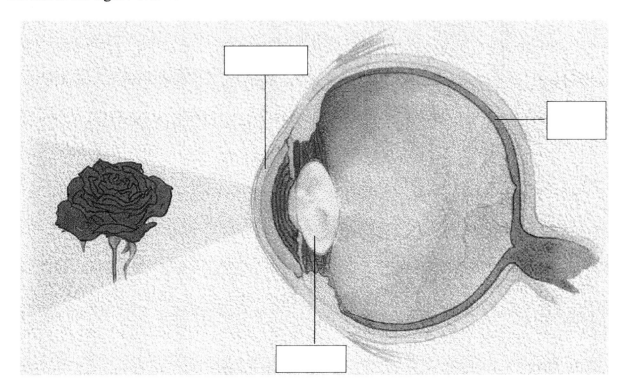

Guided Learning Questions (continued)

12. When does accommodation occur?

13. What happens to the lens when you focus on a distant object?

14. What happens to the lens when you focus on a close object?

15. Describe what nearsighted people see.

16. Why does nearsightedness occur?

17. Describe what farsighted people see.

18. Why does farsightedness occur?

Guided Learning Questions (continued)
19. What is the pupil?

20. What is the iris?

21. Label the figure below:

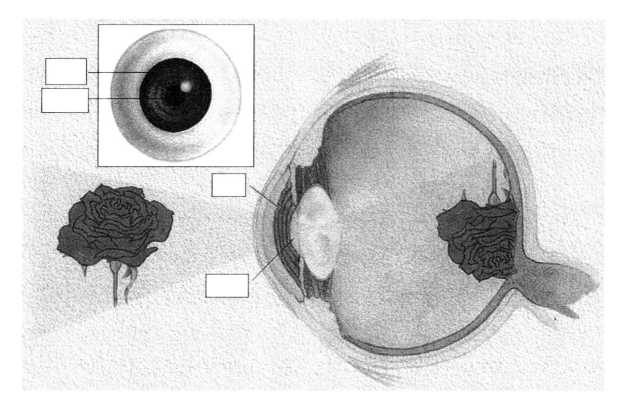

22. When does the pupil constrict?

23. What happens when the pupil constricts?

Guided Learning Questions (continued)

24. When does the pupil dilate?

25. What happens when the pupil dilates?

NAME _____   CLASS _____

Module 3b—The retina

Description
In this module, students learn how the retina converts incoming light into neural signals that are sent to the brain.

Outline
Anatomy of the retina
Rods and cones
Dark adaptation
Receptive fields
Review
Quiz
Recommended web links

Learning objectives
1. Identify the location of the retina and the optic disk.
2. Discuss the contribution of the rods and cones to visual processing.
3. Explain the processes underlying dark adaptation.
4. Discuss the operation of center-surround receptive fields.
5. Discuss the significance of lateral antagonism.

Guided Learning Questions
1. What is the retina? What does it do?

2. What (where) is the optic disk?

3. What causes the blind spot?

4. The retina contains 2 types of receptors. What are they?

Guided Learning Questions (continued)

5. What do rods play a key role in?

6. Where is the density of rods the greatest?

7. What do cones play a key role in?

8. Finish the thought: "Cones do not respond well to …"

9. Where are cones concentrated most heavily?

10. What is the fovea?

11. What is dark adaptation?

Guided Learning Questions (continued)

12. Why does the curve that charts dark adaptation consist of two segments?

13. Finish the thought: "Vision improves markedly during the first 5 -10 min as ..."

14. Finish the thought: "Further improvement ..."

15. What makes up a cell's receptive field?

16. What kind of receptive fields are particularly common?

17. Please label the figure below:

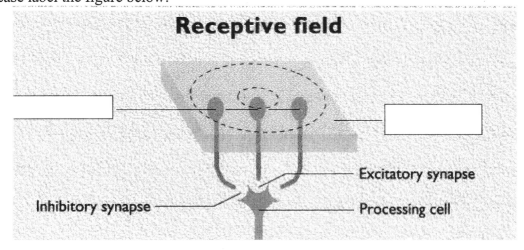

Guided Learning Questions (continued)

18. What happens when light falls on the center of the field (when you click on "center")?

19. What happens when light falls on the surround section of the field (when you click on 'surround')?

20. Which produces a higher firing rate, no light or light in both the center and surround sections of the receptive field? Explain.

21. Why are center-surround fields sensitive to contrast?

22. When does lateral antagonism occur?

NAME _____   CLASS _____

Module 3c—Vision and the brain

Description
In this module, students learn how visual signals are sent from the eye to the brain and how these signals are processed in the visual cortex.

Outline
Visual pathways
Information processing in the cortex
Bottom-up versus top-down processing
Review
Quiz
Recommended web links

Learning objectives
1. Describe the routing of signals from the eye to the brain.
2. Describe the two pathways involved in visual processing and the information they handle.
3. Describe Hubel and Wiesel's research on information processing in the visual cortex.
4. Explain the concept of feature analysis.
5. Distinguish between top-down and bottom-up processing.
6. Describe subjective contours.

Guided Learning Questions
1. Please complete the figure below:

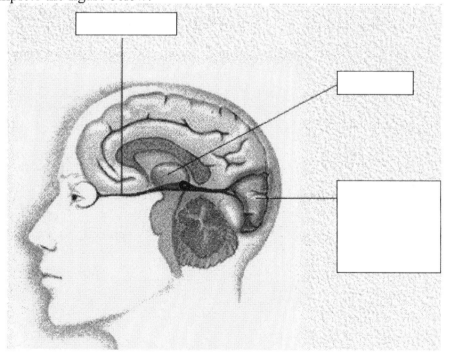

Guided Learning Questions (continued)

2. Where is the visual cortex?

3. Where is the optic chiasm?

4. Where is information from the left half of each retina sent?

5. Where is information from the right half of each retina sent?

6. Where does the Main Pathway project?

7. Where does the Secondary Pathway project?

Guided Learning Questions (continued)

8. What does the Main Pathway appear to handle?

9. What does the Secondary pathway appear to handle?

10. Why did David Hubel and Torsten Wiesel win a Nobel Prize?

11. Please complete the table below:

Major Types of Visual Cells in the Cortex

Cell type	Responds best to
Simple cells	
Complex cells	Movement of correctly oriented bars across the receptive field
	Corners, angles, or bars of a particular length moving in a particular direction

Guided Learning Questions (continued)

12. What is the key point?

13. What are feature detectors?

14. Finish the thought: "Ultimately, most visible stimuli can be represented by ..."

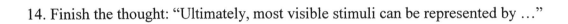

15. Describe Bottom-Up processing?

16. Describe Top-Down processing.

Guided Learning Questions (continued)

17. Complete the figure below:

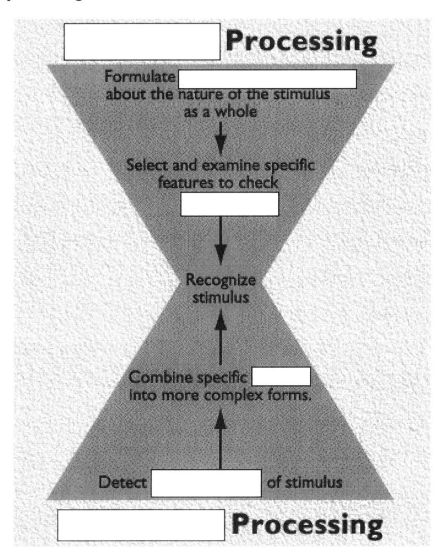

18. Why do Bottom-Up explanations of perception have problems explaining subjective contours?

NAME _____   CLASS _____

Module 3d—Perception of color

Description
In this module, the research and theory on the perception of color is discussed.

Outline
Hue, brightness, and saturation
Color mixing
Theories of color vision
Review
Quiz
Recommended web links

Learning objectives
1. Describe the color solid.
2. Distinguish between subtractive and additive color mixing.
3. Describe the trichromatic and opponent process theories of color vision.
4. Discuss the modern reconciliation of the trichromatic and opponent process theories.

Guided Learning Questions
1. Please complete the figure below:

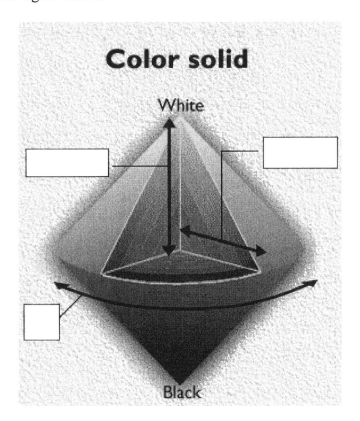

Guided Learning Questions (continued)

2. Please complete the table below:

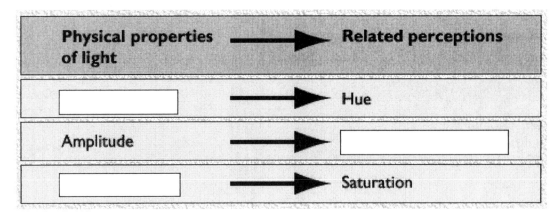

3. What are the 2 types of color mixing?

4. How does subtractive color mixing work?

5. How does additive color mixing work?

6. Which type of color mixing is most like human perception?

Guided Learning Questions (continued)
7. Describe the Trichromatic Theory of color processing.

8. How can people see diverse colors?

9. What are complimentary colors?

10. What is an after image?

Guided Learning Questions (continued)

11. What does the afterimage of the flag look like?

12. Describe the Opponent Process theory of color vision.

13. What are the 3 pairs of opponent colors posited?

14. Which of the two theories of color vision is correct? Explain.

15. Is there a biological basis for opponent processes? Explain.

NAME _____   CLASS _____

Module 3e—Gestalt psychology

Description
In this module, students learn about various principles of form perception that were developed by Gestalt psychologists.

Outline
Phi phenomenon
Figure and ground
Gestalt principles
Review
Quiz
Recommended web links

Learning objectives
1. Discuss the origins and the basic premise of Gestalt psychology.
2. Describe the phi phenomenon and the distinction between figure and ground.
3. Explain the Gestalt principles of proximity and similarity.
4. Explain the Gestalt principles of continuity, closure, and good form.

Guided Learning Questions
1. What were Gestalt psychologists interested in?

2. What is the basic principle of Gestalt psychology?

3. What is the Phi Phenomenon?

Guided Learning Questions (continued)

4. Finish the thought: "Dividing visual displays into figure and ground …"

5. What is the figure?

6. What is the ground?

7. Describe the following:

       Proximity principle -

       Similarity principle -

       Continuity principle -

       Closure principle -

       Law of Good form –

NAME _____   CLASS _____

Module 3f—Depth perception

Description
In this module, students learn about the visual cues that allow one to perceive depth or distance.

Outline
Depth perception
Types of depth cues
Monocular cues
Binocular cues
Review
Quiz
Recommended web links

Learning objectives
1. Distinguish between monocular and binocular cues in depth perception.
2. Describe the pictorial cues of interposition and relative size.
3. Describe the pictorial cues of linear perspective and texture gradients.
4. Describe the pictorial cues of height in plane and light and shadow.
5. Describe accommodation.
6. Describe the binocular cues of convergence and retinal disparity.

Guided Learning Questions
1. What does depth perception involve?

2. What are the two types of depth cues?

3. What are monocular depth cues?

Guided Learning Questions (continued)
4. What are the 2 kinds of monocular depth cues?

5. What are pictorial depth cues?

6. Describe how each of the following cue depth information:

Interposition -

Relative size -

Linear perspective -

Texture gradient -

Light and shadow -

Height in plane -

Guided Learning Questions (continued)

7. Describe how the active use of the eyes allows each of the following to provide depth information:

Accommodation -

Motion parallax -

8. What are binocular depth cues?

9. What is the principal binocular depth cue?

10. Describe the relationship between distance (depth) and retinal disparity.

11. What is convergence?

12. Describe the relationship between distance (depth) and convergence.

NAME _____   CLASS _____

Module 3g—Visual illusions

Description
In this module, students see some optical illusions and discuss their origins.

Outline
Geometric illusions
The Ames room
Impossible figures
The moon illusion
Review
Quiz
Simulation – The Poggendorff Illusion
Recommended web links

Learning objectives
1. Explain the basis for the Müller-Lyer illusion.
2. Explain the basis for the Ponzo illusion.
3. Describe several other geometric illusions.
4. Describe the illusion seen in the Ames room.
5. Describe the concept of impossible figures and the moon illusion.

Guided Learning Questions
1. What does an optical illusion involve?

2. What causes the Müller-Lyer illusion?

Guided Learning Questions (continued)

3. What causes the Ponzo illusion?

4. What is the Ames room?

5. What are impossible figures?

6. Finish the thought: "The initial illusion that impossible figures make sense…"

Guided Learning Questions (continued)

7. What is the moon illusion? What causes the moon illusion?

8. What do optical illusions reveal about visual perception?

NAME _____   CLASS _____

Module 3h—The sense of hearing

Description
In this module, students learn how the ear converts sounds into neural impulses that are sent to the brain.

Outline
Characteristics of sound
Human hearing capacities
Sensory processing in the ear
Review
Quiz
Recommended web links

Learning objectives
1. List the three properties of sound and the aspects of auditory perception that they influence.
2. Summarize information on human hearing capacities.
3. Describe how sensory processing occurs in the ear.

Guided Learning Questions
1. Complete the table below:

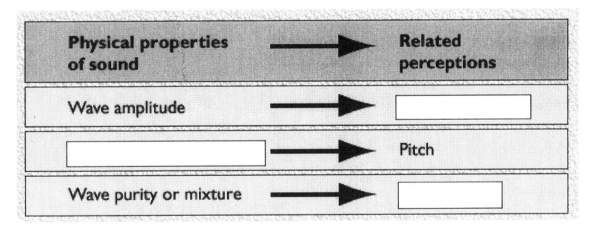

2. Finish the thought: "For the most part, higher frequencies are perceived as …"

3. Humans can hear sounds ranging from a low of _____ hertz up to about _____ hertz.

Guided Learning Questions (continued)

4. The human ear is most sensitive to sounds with frequencies between _____ hertz and

_____ hertz.

5. Finish the thought: "In general, the greater the amplitude of the sound waves....."

6. What unit is used to measure amplitude?

7. Finish the thought: "A general rule is that..."

8. What is the decibel level of "Rock concert in front of speakers"?

9. Brief exposure to sounds over _____ can be painful.

10. What does purity of a sound influence?

11. The human ear can be divided into 3 parts. What are they?

Guided Learning Questions (continued)

12. What is the pinna?

13. What do the hammer, anvil, and stirrup do?

14. What is the cochlea?

15. What structures are inside the cochlea?

16. What causes hair cells to fire?

17. What do hair cells do?

NAME _____   CLASS _____

Module 4a—Biological rhythms

Description
In this module, students see how biological rhythms modulate our cycles of sleep and arousal.

Outline
Biological rhythms in humans
Circadian rhythms and sleep
Circadian rhythms and jet lag
Circadian rhythms and rotating shifts
Review
Quiz
Recommended web links

Learning Objectives
1. Describe four time cycles in humans.
2. Summarize what is known about our biological clocks and their relationship to sleep.
3. Describe research on how to make shift rotation less disruptive.

Guided Learning Questions
1. What are biological rhythms?

2. What 4 time cycles are related to behavior in humans?

1:

2:

3:

4:

3. Finish the thought: "Circadian rhythms also produce variations in...."

Guided Learning Questions (continued)

4. What happens to people who spend weeks living in a cave, cut off from clocks and the cycle of day and night?

5. Why do theorists believe that the cycle of day and night is important?

6. What does exposure to light affect?

7. What is the key cause of jet lag?

8. How long does it usually take for psychomotor performance to recover if you fly eastward? Westward?

9. Why do people adjust more easily to westward travel?

Guided Learning Questions (continued)
10. What do shift work studies show about rotating shifts?

11. Finish the thought: "Research by Charles Czeisler and his colleagues has shown that shift rotation can be less disruptive when…."

12. What else did they show?

NAME _____   CLASS _____

Module 4b—Sleep

Description
In this module, students learn about the various stages of sleep and how people cycle through them as they sleep.

Outline
Conducting sleep research
Stages of sleep
Repeating the cycle
Age trends in sleep
Review
Quiz
Recommended web links

Learning Objectives
1. Describe how sleep research is conducted.
2. Describe how the sleep cycle evolves through the night.
3. Compare and contrast REM and NREM sleep.
4. Summarize age trends in patterns of sleep.

Guided Learning Questions
1. What is an EEG? What does it do?

2. Human brainwaves are usually divided into 4 principal bands. What are they?

1:

2:

3:

4:

Guided Learning Questions (continued)
3. What are Beta waves?

4. What are Alpha waves?

5. What are Theta waves?

6. What are Delta waves?

7. What happens as you descend through stages 1, 2, 3 and 4 of the sleep cycle?

8. What is Stage 1 sleep?

9. What happens during Stage 2 sleep?

Guided Learning Questions (continued)

10. What are Stages 3 and 4 called? Why?

11. What happens after about a half-hour in these deep stages of sleep?

12. What happens when you reach what should be Stage 1 again?

13. What does REM stand for?

14. Finish the thought: "Although REM us a deep stage of sleep, EEG activity …"

15. What did William Dement find?

16. What are the characteristics of REM sleep?

17. How does the sleep cycle change across the night?

18. When does the most REM sleep and dreaming occur?

19. Describe the sleep time patterns for someone that is:

Newborn-2 years old -

About 3 years old -

Guided Learning Questions (continued)

An adolescent -

An adult -

An elderly adult –

NAME _____   CLASS _____

Module 4c—Abused drugs and their effects

Description
In this module, the effects and risks of five categories of recreational drugs are discussed.

Outline
Narcotics
Sedatives
Stimulants
Hallucinogens
Cannabis
Review
Quiz
Recommended web links

Learning Objectives
1. Summarize the effects and risks of narcotic drugs.
2. Summarize the effects and risks of sedatives.
3. Summarize the effects and risks of stimulants.
4. Summarize the effects and risks of hallucinogens.
5. Summarize the effects and risks of cannabis.

Guided learning Questions
1. What are some examples of narcotic drugs?

2. How are narcotic drugs ingested?

3. What are the desired effects of narcotic drugs?

Guided Learning Questions (continued)

4. Do narcotic drug users face a high risk of psychological dependence? What about physical dependence?

5. What other risks do narcotic drug users face?

6. Do narcotic drug users face additional risks of prolonged use?

7. What are some examples of sedatives?

8. How are sedatives ingested?

9. What are the desired effects of sedatives?

Guided Learning Questions (continued)

10. Do sedative users face a high risk of psychological dependence? What about physical dependence?

11. What other risks do sedative users face?

12. Do sedative users face additional risks of prolonged use?

13. What are some examples of stimulants?

14. How are stimulants ingested?

15. What are the desired effects of stimulants?

Guided Learning Questions (continued)

16. Do stimulant users face a high risk of psychological dependence? What about physical dependence?

17. What other risks do stimulant users face?

18. Do stimulant users face additional risks of prolonged use?

19. What are some examples of hallucinogens?

20. How are hallucinogens ingested?

21. What are the desired effects of hallucinogens?

Guided Learning Questions (continued)

22. Do hallucinogen users face a high risk of psychological dependence? What about physical dependence?

23. What other risks do hallucinogen users face?

24. Do hallucinogen users face additional risks of prolonged use?

25. What are some examples of cannabis?

26. How is cannabis ingested?

27. What are the desired effects of cannabis?

28. Do cannabis users face a high risk of psychological dependence? What about physical dependence?

Guided Learning Questions (continued)

29. What other risks do cannabis users face?

30. Do cannabis users face additional risks of prolonged use?

NAME _____   CLASS _____

Module 4d—Drugs and synaptic transmission

Description
In this module, students learn how various drugs exert their effects by altering neurotransmitter activity in the brain.

Outline
General mechanisms of action
Cocaine and amphetamines
Valium and opiates
LSD and marijuana
Review
Quiz
Recommended web links

Learning Objectives
1. Describe the many ways in which drugs can alter neurotransmitter activity at the synapse.
2. Describe the effects of cocaine and amphetamines on neurotransmitter activity.
3. Describe the effects of valium and opiates on neurotransmitter activity.
4. Describe the effects of LSD and marijuana on neurotransmitter activity.

Guided learning Questions
1. How do psychoactive drugs work?

2. What are neurotransmitters?

3. How do drugs influence the synthesis process?

Guided Learning Questions (continued)

4. How do drugs influence the release process?

5. How do drugs influence the reuptake process?

6. How do drugs influence the inactivation process?

7. How do drugs influence the binding process?

8. What kinds of synapses are affected by cocaine or amphetamines?

9. How does cocaine affect synaptic transmission?

Guided Learning Questions (continued)
10. How do amphetamines affect synaptic transmission?

11. What causes the emotional crash experienced by many cocaine and amphetamine users?

12. How do traditional antianxiety drugs affect synaptic transmission?

13. How do heroine, morphine, and other opiates affect synaptic transmission?

14. How does LSD affect synaptic transmission?

15. Where have receptors activated by THC been found?

NAME _____   CLASS _____

Module 5a—Overview of classical conditioning

Description
In this module, students learn how classical conditioning governs many reflex responses.

Outline
Pavlov's demonstration
Terminology
Classical conditioning in everyday life
Review
Quiz
Recommended web links

Learning Objectives
1. Describe Pavlov's demonstration of classical conditioning.
2. Describe the key elements in classical conditioning.
3. Discuss how classical conditioning may shape phobias, other emotional responses, and physiological processes.

Guided Learning Questions
1. What is classical conditioning?

2. What did Pavlov notice about dogs that had become accustomed to his research procedure?

3. What did Pavlov do to investigate further?

4. How did the dog respond to the tone after the tone and the meat powder were presented together a number of times?

Guided Learning Questions (continued)

5. How did Pavlov change the tone from a neutral stimulus to one that elicited salivation?

6. Please define the following:

UCS -

UCR -

CS -

CR -

7. Complete the figure below:

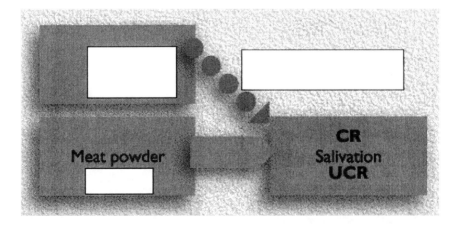

Guided Learning Questions (continued)

8. According to classical conditioning, why do people cringe at the sound of a dentist's drill? What is the UCS? What is the CS? What is the UCR? What is the CR?

9. How do advertisers take advantage of classical conditioning?

10. What is immunosuppression? How can one classically condition an immunosuppressive response? What is the UCS? What is the CS? What is the UCR? What is the CR?

Module 5b—Basic processes in classical conditioning

Description
In this module, basic processes in classical conditioning are discussed to expand on the rich complexity of this form of learning.

Outline
Acquisition and extinction
Spontaneous recovery
Generalization and discrimination
Higher-order conditioning
Review
Quiz
Recommended web links

Learning Objectives
1. Describe the classical conditioning phenomena of acquisition, extinction, and spontaneous recovery.
2. Describe the processes of generalization and discrimination.
3. Summarize the classic study of Little Albert.
4. Explain what happens in higher-order conditioning.

Guided Learning Questions
1. What is acquisition?

2. How does the strength of the dog's conditioned response change across acquisition trials?

3. What is extinction?

4. What leads to the extinction of a conditioned response?

Guided Learning Questions (continued)

5. What is spontaneous recovery?

6. How did the dog respond to the tone after Pavlov gave the dog a 24 hr. rest?

7. What is the practical meaning of spontaneous recovery?

8. When does stimulus generalization occur?

9. Please complete the figure below:

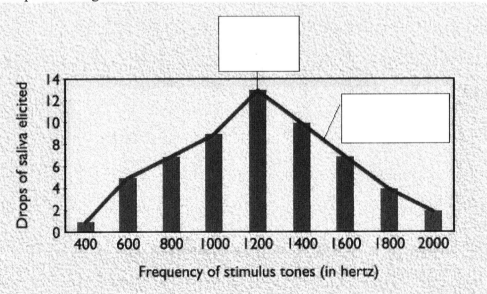

With respect to generalization, what does this figure show?

Guided Learning Questions (continued)
10. Describe the "Little Albert" study.

11. Did Albert's fear response generalize? Explain.

12. What is stimulus discrimination?

13. What happens to the shape of the generalization gradient with learning?

14. What is the basic principle that governs stimulus discrimination?

15. What is higher-order conditioning? When does it occur?

16. What does higher-order conditioning show?

NAME _____   CLASS _____

Module 5c—Overview of operant conditioning

Description
In this module, the basic principles of operant conditioning are discussed.

Outline
Terminology and procedures
Acquisition and shaping
Extinction
Review
Quiz
Recommended web links
Simulation –Shaping in Operant Conditioning

Learning Objectives
1. Describe Skinner's principle of reinforcement and the prototype experimental procedures used in studies of operant conditioning.
2. Describe the operant conditioning phenomena of acquisition and shaping.
3. Describe extinction in operant conditioning and explain the importance of resistance to extinction.

Guided Learning Questions
1. What is operant conditioning?

2. When does reinforcement occur?

3. Provide a real-world example of reinforcement.

Guided Learning Questions (continued)
4. What is a Skinner box?

5. What is the primary dependent variable in most research on operant conditioning?

6. What is a cumulative recorder? What does it do?

7. What is the key consideration when interpreting cumulative recorder graphs?

8. What kind of slope is produced by a rapid and steady response?

9. What kind of slope is produced by an increasing response rate?

Guided Learning Questions (continued)
10. What kind of slope is produced by a decreasing response rate?

11. What is acquisition?

12. What is shaping?

13. What is extinction in operant conditioning?

14. Finish the thought: "The greater the resistance to extinction…"

NAME _____   CLASS _____

Module 5d—Schedules of reinforcement

Description
In this module, students learn how schedules of reinforcement influence patterns of operant responding.

Outline
Continuous versus intermittent reinforcement
Types of intermittent reinforcement
Effects of intermittent schedules
Review
Quiz
Recommended web links

Learning Objectives
1. Distinguish between continuous and intermittent reinforcement.
2. Distinguish between fixed-ratio, variable-ratio, fixed-interval, and variable-interval schedules of reinforcement.
3. Discuss how various schedules of reinforcement affect patterns of responding.

Guided Learning Questions
1. When does continuous reinforcement occur?

2. When does intermittent (or partial) reinforcement occur?

3. Which schedule of reinforcement leads to longer lasting effects?

4. What are the two types of intermittent reinforcement schedules?

Guided Learning Questions (continued)

5. Describe ratio schedules.

6. Describe interval schedules.

7. Please complete the table below:

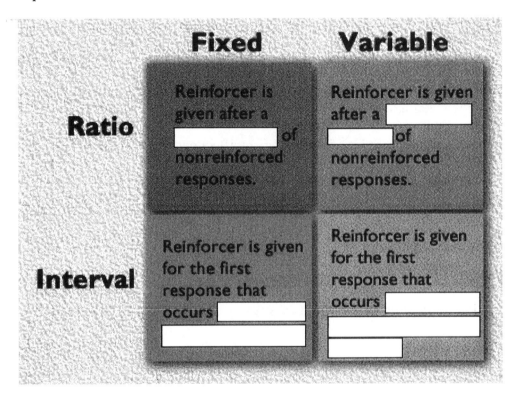

8. Provide an example of a fixed-ratio schedule.

Guided Learning Questions (continued)

9. Provide an example of a variable-ratio schedule.

10. Provide an example of a fixed-interval schedule.

11. Provide an example of a variable-interval schedule.

12. In general, which schedules tends to produce more rapid responding? Why?

13. Which schedules lead to greater resistance to extinction?

14. Which schedules tend to generate more stable response rates?

15. Which schedule shows a "scalloped" response curve? Why?

NAME _____ CLASS _____

Module 5e—Reinforcement and punishment

Description
In this module, the differences between positive reinforcement, negative reinforcement, and punishment are explained.

Outline
Positive reinforcement
Negative reinforcement
Punishment
Review
Quiz
Recommended web links

Learning Objectives
1. Explain the nature and effects of positive reinforcement.
2. Explain the nature and effects of negative reinforcement.
3. Explain the nature and effects of punishment.

Guided learning Questions
1. What are the two forms of reinforcement?

1:

2:

2. Please complete the table below:

Process	Behavior	Consequence	Effect on behavior
Negative reinforcement	Make response	Aversive stimulus	Tendency to make response
Positive reinforcement	Make response	Rewarding stimulus presented	Tendency to make response
Punishment	Make response	Aversive stimulus	Tendency to make response

Guided Learning Questions (continued)

3. Provide a real word example of each of the following:

Positive reinforcement –

Negative reinforcement –

Punishment –

4. What is the difference between negative reinforcement and punishment?

5. Why is the concept of punishment in operant conditioning confusing to many students?

1:

2:

NAME _____   CLASS _____

Module 5f—Avoidance and escape learning

Description
In this module, students learn how avoidance behavior involves both classical conditioning and operant conditioning.

Outline
Escape learning
Avoidance learning
Two-process theory of avoidance
Review
Quiz
Recommended web links

Learning Objectives
1. Describe and distinguish between escape learning and avoidance learning.
2. Explain Mowrer's two-process theory and the role of negative reinforcement in avoidance behavior.
3. Explain why phobias are thought to be so resistant to extinction.

Guided Learning Questions
1. What does escape learning involve?

2. Please complete the table below:

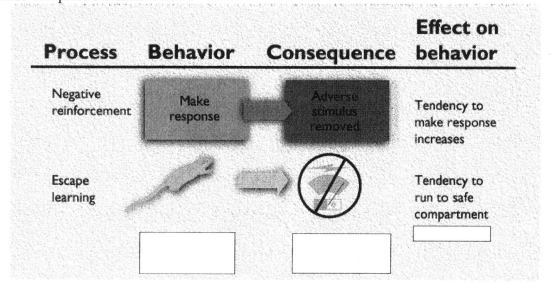

Process	Behavior	Consequence	Effect on behavior
Negative reinforcement	Make response	Adverse stimulus removed	Tendency to make response increases
Escape learning			Tendency to run to safe compartment

Guided Learning Questions (continued)

3. Give an everyday example of escape learning.

4. What does avoidance learning involve?

5. What role does classical conditioning play in Mowrer's two-process theory of avoidance learning?

6. According to the theory, what serves as the conditioned stimulus?

Guided Learning Questions (continued)

7. What role does operant conditioning play in the two process theory of avoidance learning? What role does negative reinforcement play in the process?

8. Why are phobias resistant to extinction?

1:

2:

NAME _____   CLASS _____

Module 6a—Memory encoding

Description
In this module, students see how the encoding of information plays a crucial role in memory.

Outline
Types of encoding
Levels-of-processing theory
Encoding with visual imagery
Mnemonic devices
Review
Quiz
Recommended web links
Simulation – Memory Processes I

Learning Objectives
1. Distinguish between encoding, storage, and retrieval in memory.
2. Distinguish between structural, phonemic, and semantic encoding and their relationship to memory.
3. Discuss the effects of visual imagery on memory.
4. Describe the link method and method of loci.

Guided Learning Questions
1. What does encoding involve?

2. What does storage involve?

3. What does retrieval involve?

4. Why do most people have difficulty identifying the penny?

5. Finish the thought: "According to Fergus Craik and Robert Lockhart..."

6. Please complete the table below:

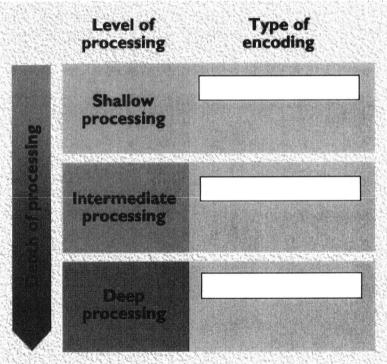

7. What does structural encoding involve?

Guided Learning Questions (continued)
8. What does phonemic encoding involve?

9. What does semantic encoding involve?

10. What is the predicted relationship between depth of processing and duration of memory?

11. Give an example of a question that would induce structural encoding?

12. Give an example of a question that would induce phonemic encoding?

13. Give an example of a question that would induce semantic encoding?

14. Did the results of Craik and Tulving's experiment support Craik and Lockhart's levels-of-processing idea? Explain.

Guided Learning Questions (continued)

15. What did Allan Pavio do?

16. What did his results show?

17. According to Pavio, why does imagery facilitate memory?

18. How does the link method work?

19. How does the method of loci work?

NAME _____   CLASS _____

Module 6b—Memory storage

Description
In this module, students learn how information is stored in memory.

Outline
Sensory memory
Short-term memory
Long-term memory
Organizational devices in LTM
Review
Quiz
Recommended web links
Simulation – Memory Processes II

Learning Objectives
1. Describe the role of the sensory store in memory.
2. Discuss the characteristics of short-term memory.
3. Describe Baddeley's model of working memory.
4. Describe conceptual hierarchies, semantic networks, schemas, and their role in long-term memory.

Guided Learning Questions
1. Please complete the figure below:

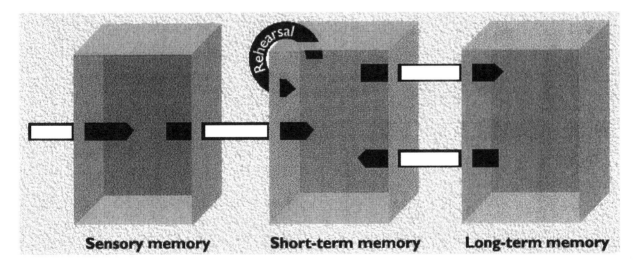

Guided Learning Questions (continued)

2. What did George Sperling demonstrate?

3. What was the independent variable in Sperling's experiment?

4. What did Sperling's results indicate about the decay of the sensory memory trace?

5. What is short-term memory?

6. What is rehearsal?

7. Why do mistakes in short-term memory experiments involve acoustical confusions?

Guided Learning Questions (continued)

8. What is the duration of short-term storage when people cannot rehearse?

9. How many items can short-term memory hold?

10. What is a chunk?

11. According to Alan Baddeley, working memory consists of three components. What are they? Please complete the figure below:

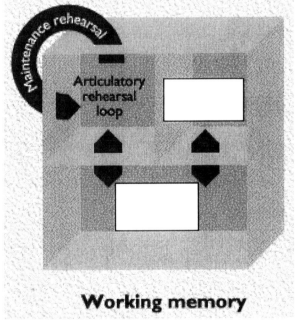

Guided Learning Questions (continued)

12. What does the executive control system do?

13. What does the visuo-spatial sketchpad do?

14. What does the articulatory rehearsal loop do?

15. What is long-term memory?

16. What is a conceptual hierarchy?

Guided Learning Questions (continued)

17. What is a semantic network?

18. What is a schema?

19. Did you pick any objects that were not in the office? If so, which ones?

20. What did Brewer and Treyens find?

NAME _____   CLASS _____

Module 6c—Physiology of memory

Description
In this module, the physiological underpinnings of memory are discussed.

Outline
Biochemistry of memory
Neural circuitry of memory
Anatomy of memory
Review
Quiz
Recommended web links

Learning Objectives
1. Describe how alterations in synaptic transmission may contribute to memory.
2. Summarize evidence on the neural circuitry underlying memory.
3. Distinguish between anterograde and retrograde amnesia.
4. Describe the case of H. M. and its implications regarding the anatomical structures involved in memory.

Guided Learning Questions
1. What did Wilder Penfield do in the 1960's and what did he find?

2. What did further study reveal?

Guided Learning Questions (continued)

3. What has research by Erik Kandel and colleagues shown about specific forms of learning in the sea slug?

4. What does Kandel believe?

5. Finish the thought: "Among other things, Alzheimer's disease appears to be associated with..."

6. What did Richard Thompson and his colleagues show?

7. In some cases, memory formation may stimulate neural growth. Explain.

8. What are the two types of organic amnesia?

Guided Learning Questions (continued)

9. Describe retrograde amnesia.

10. Describe anterograde amnesia.

11. Who was H.M.? What caused his amnesia?

12. Hippocampal damage has a severe impact on _____ .

The _____ may be largely unaffected.

13. What does the declarative memory system handle?

Guided Learning Questions (continued)

14. What does the procedural memory system handle?

15. Are most memories housed in the hippocampus? Explain.

NAME _____   CLASS _____

Module 6d—Problem solving

Description
In this module, students learn about different categories of problems and the barriers that can prevent effective problem solving.

Outline
Types of problems
Barriers to solving problems
Review
Quiz
Recommended web links
Simulation – Problem Solving

Learning Objectives
1. List and describe the three types of problems proposed by Greeno.
2. Explain how irrelevant information and functional fixedness can hinder problem solving.
3. Explain how mental set and unnecessary constraints can hinder problem solving.

Guided Learning Questions
1. What does "Problem solving" refer to?

2. Jim Greeno has proposed that problems can be categorized into 3 basic classes. What are they?

1:

2:

3:

4. Describe problems of inducing structure.

Guided Learning Questions (continued)

4. Describe problems of arrangement.

5. Describe problems of transformation.

6. How does irrelevant information interfere with problem solving?

7. What is functional fixedness?

8. What is a mental set? How can it interfere with problem solving?

9. How do assumptions about constraints interfere with problem solving?

NAME _____ CLASS _____

Module 6e—Decision making

Description
In this module, students examine some of the factors that influence decision making processes.

Outline
Basic heuristics
Ignoring base rates
The conjunctive fallacy
The gambler's fallacy
The law of small numbers
Overestimating the improbable
Overconfidence effects
Framing effects
Review
Quiz
Recommended web links

Learning Objectives
1. Describe the Availability and Representativeness heuristics.
2. Describe the Conjunction fallacy and the Gambler's fallacy.
3. Discuss the Law of Small Numbers
4. Explain how the availability heuristic causes people to overestimate the likelihood of unlikely events.
5. Describe overconfidence effects.
6. Discuss how positive or negative wording can influence judgments.

Guided Learning Questions
1. What does decision making involve?

2. According to Simon, why do people make seemingly irrational decisions?

Guided Learning Questions (continued)

3. What does risky decision making involve?

4. What are heuristics?

5. What is the availability heuristic?

6. What is the representativeness heuristic?

7. When does the conjunction fallacy occur?

8. What is the gambler's fallacy?

Guided Learning Questions (continued)

9. What is the law of small numbers?

10. Why do people tend to overestimate the improbable? Does the availability heuristic play a role in this? Explain.

11. What is the overconfidence effect?

12. Explain how framing affects judgment.

NAME _____   CLASS _____

Module 7a—Types of psychological tests

Description
In this module, students learn about the types of tests routinely used by psychologists.

Outline
Tests of mental abilities
Personality tests
Review
Quiz
Recommended web links

Learning objectives
1. List and describe the principal categories of psychological tests.
2. Distinguish between intelligence, aptitude, and achievement tests.
3. Describe some representative personality tests.

Guided Learning Questions
1. What is a psychological test? What do psychological tests measure?

2. What are the two broad categories of psychological tests?

      1:

      2:

3. What kind of test is the most common kind of psychological test?

Guided Learning Questions (continued)

4. What are the three subcategories of mental ability tests?

      1:

      2:

      3:

5. What do intelligence tests measure?

6. What are two examples of prominent intelligence tests?

      1:

      2:

7. What do aptitude tests measure?

8. What eight abilities does the Differential Aptitude Test measure?

      1:                        5:

      2:                        6:

      3:                        7:

      4:                        8:

Guided Learning Questions (continued)
9. What do achievement tests measure?

10. What are the two broad subcategories of personality tests?

    1:

    2:

11. What are self-report inventories?

12. What do norms represent?

13. What do projective tests ask subjects to do?

14. Name two projective tests.

    1:

    2:

NAME _____   CLASS _____

Module 7b—Key concepts in testing

Description
In this module, students learn how psychologists assess the reliability and validity of psychological tests.

Outline
Standardization
Reliability
Validity
Review
Quiz
Recommended web links
Simulation – Psychological Testing: Measuring Your Creativity

Learning objectives
1. Explain the concepts of standardization and test norms.
2. Explain the meaning of test reliability and how it is estimated.
3. Explain the three types of validity and how they are assessed.

Guided Learning Questions
1. What does "standardization" mean?

2. What do test norms tell us?

3. What does percentile score indicate?

4. What does a percentile score of 81 mean?

Guided Learning Questions (continued)

5. What is reliability?

6. How is test-retest reliability estimated?

7. What is a correlation coefficient?

8. Finish the thought: "If people get fairly similar scores..."

9. Finish the thought: "The closer the correlation coefficient comes to +1.00..."

10. What is the reliability coefficient of the Stanford-Binet Intelligence Test? What does this indicate about the scale's reliability?

11. What is validity?

Guided Learning Questions (continued)

12. What are the three types of validity discussed?

      1:

      2:

      3:

13. What is content validity?

14. What is criterion validity?

15. What is construct validity?

NAME _____ CLASS _____

Module 7c—Understanding IQ scores

Description
In this module, the evolution of intelligence testing is discussed and students learn the meaning of modern IQ scores.

Outline
Binet's breakthrough
Terman and the Stanford-Binet
Wechsler's innovations
The meaning of modern IQ scores
Review
Quiz
Recommended web links

Learning objectives
1. Summarize the contributions of Binet to the evolution of intelligence testing.
2. Summarize the contributions of Terman to the evolution of intelligence testing.
3. Summarize the contributions of Wechsler to the evolution of intelligence testing.
4. Explain the meaning of an individual's score on a modern intelligence test.

Guided Learning Questions
1. Who developed the first successful intelligence test?

2. What is "mental age"?

3. What does IQ stand for? How is IQ calculated?

Guided Learning Questions (continued)

4. What does an intelligence quotient of 100 mean?

5. What is the IQ of a 9-yr.-old with a mental age of 6? With a mental age of 12?

6. What did Wechsler find?

7. Finish the thought: "To highlight the distinction between verbal and non-verbal ability..."

8. What is a normal distribution?

9. What percentage of the scores fall within:

   ± 1 standard deviation of the mean?

   ± 2 standard deviations of the mean?

   ± 3 standard deviations of the mean?

Guided Learning Questions (continued)
10. What does an IQ score of 115 mean?

11. What does an IQ score of 100 mean?

12. What does an IQ score of 85 mean?

13. What percentage of the population scores lower than:

    85 on an IQ test?

    100 on an IQ test?

    115 on an IQ test?

    130 on an IQ test?

14. Please complete the figure below:

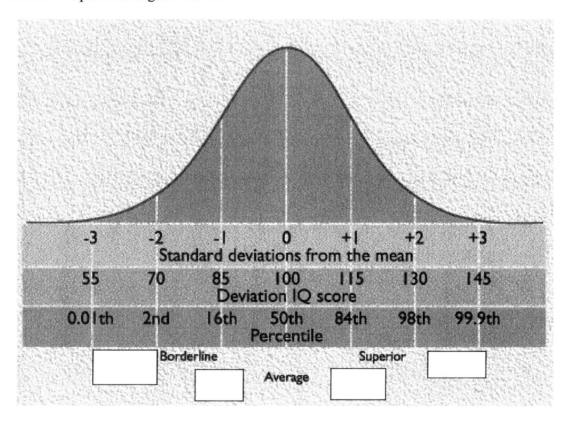

NAME _____ CLASS _____

Module 7d—Heredity, environment, and intelligence

Description
In this module, the methods that researchers use to explore the nature versus nurture issue are examined, and data on the determinants of intelligence are discussed.

Outline
Family studies
Twin studies
Adoption studies
Estimating heritability
Reaction range
Review
Quiz
Recommended web links

Learning objectives
1. Distinguish between family studies, twin studies, and adoption studies.
2. Summarize the empirical evidence that heredity affects intelligence.
3. Discuss contemporary estimates of the heritability of intelligence.
4. Using the concept of reaction range, explain how heredity and the environment interact to affect intelligence.

Guided Learning Questions
1. What are the three most important methods used to disentangle the affects of heredity and environment?

    1:

    2:

    3:

2. Describe family studies.

3. What do the results of family studies show?

Guided Learning Questions (continued)

4. Why can't family studies provide conclusive evidence that a trait is influenced by heredity?

5. Describe twin studies.

6. What is the genetic relatedness of identical twins? What is the genetic relatedness of fraternal twins?

7. What do the results of twin studies show?

8. What do critics argue?

Guided Learning Questions (continued)
9. Describe adoption studies.

10. What do the results of adoption studies show?

11. Is there evidence for the influence of environmental factors on IQ? Explain.

12. What is a heritability ratio?

13. What is the consensus estimate of the heritability of intelligence?

14. What is a reaction range?

15. According to the reaction range model, how does the quality of the environment affect intelligence scores?

NAME _____   CLASS _____

Module 8a—Hunger

Description
In this module, some of the biological and environmental factors that regulate hunger and eating are explained.

Outline
Biological factors
Social factors
Review
Quiz
Recommended web links

Learning objectives
1. Summarize evidence on the areas of the brain implicated in the regulation of hunger.
2. Summarize evidence on how fluctuations in blood glucose and insulin affect hunger.
3. Summarize evidence on how various environmental factors influence hunger.

Guided Learning Questions
1. Which area of the brain controls the experience of hunger?

2. Complete the table below:

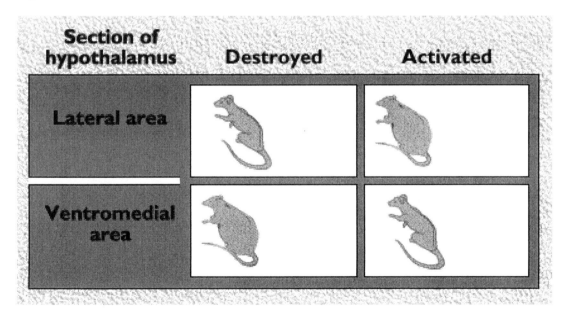

Guided Learning Questions (continued)

3. Given these results, what did theorists conclude?

4. Why were these ideas challenged?

5. Finish the thought: "The dual-center model…"

6. Complete the table below:

Factors That Play a Role in the Hunger Regulation System

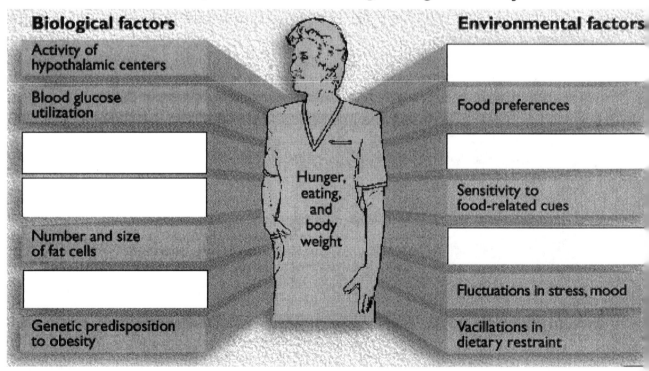

Biological factors		Environmental factors
Activity of hypothalamic centers		
Blood glucose utilization		Food preferences
	Hunger, eating, and body weight	
		Sensitivity to food-related cues
Number and size of fat cells		
		Fluctuations in stress, mood
Genetic predisposition to obesity		Vacillations in dietary restraint

Guided Learning Questions (continued)

7. What happens to hunger when the body's blood glucose level increases? When it decreases?

8. What are glucostats? What do they do?

9. What is insulin? What happens when the body's insulin level rises?

10. Explain how observational learning can affect eating behavior.

11. What did Stanley Schachter find in his time cue study?

12. What did Stanley Schachter find in his ice cream study?

Guided Learning Questions (continued)
13. What did Judith Rodin find?

14. How does stress affect eating behavior?

NAME _____ CLASS _____

Module 8b—Achievement motivation

Description
In this module, students learn about the achievement motive and how it shapes behavior.

Outline
Measuring the need for achievement
Characteristics of people with high need for achievement
Situational determinants of achievement behavior
Review
Quiz
Recommended web links

Learning objectives
1. Describe the achievement motive and how the TAT has been used to measure it.
2. Discuss how individual differences in the need for achievement influence behavior.
3. Explain how situational factors affect achievement strivings.

Guided Learning Questions
1. What is achievement motivation?

2. Where is achievement motivation found in Maslow's hierarchy?

3. How is need for achievement usually measured?

Guided Learning Questions (continued)

4. What does TAT stand for? What is the TAT?

5. Who is David McClelland and what did he do?

6. Describe individuals who score high in need for achievement.

7. What does John Atkinson theorize?

Guided Learning Questions (continued)

8. According to Atkinson, what are the three situational factors that affect achievement behavior?

    1:

    2:

    3:

9. Explain why high achievers prefer tasks of intermediate difficulty.

NAME _____   CLASS _____

Module 8c—Elements of emotion

Description
In this module, students learn about the nature of emotions and the physiological structures and processes that regulate them.

Outline
The cognitive component
The physiological component
The behavioral component
Review
Quiz
Recommended web links

Learning objectives
1. Describe the cognitive component of emotion.
2. Describe how the autonomic nervous system and areas in the brain regulate emotions.
3. Discuss the nature and validity of polygraph tests.
4. Discuss the body language of emotions and the facial feedback hypothesis.

Guided Learning Questions
1. What are the three components of emotion?

      1:

      2:

      3:

2. What does the cognitive component involve?

3. What does the physiological component involve?

Guided Learning Questions (continued)

4. What does the autonomic nervous system do?

5. What are the two divisions of the autonomic nervous system?

     1:

     2:

6. What does the sympathetic division do? How?

7. What does the parasympathetic division do? How?

8. Which brain structures are viewed as the seat of emotion?

9. Can the polygraph detect lies? What can it detect?

Guided Learning Questions (continued)
10. Can the polygraph be wrong? Explain.

11. What does the behavioral component of emotion involve?

12. Which six emotions can people identify based on facial cues?

    1:                              4:

    2:                              5:

    3:                              6:

13. What is the facial feedback hypothesis?

14. Is there cross-cultural agreement on the identification of emotion based on facial features? What does this suggest?

NAME _____   CLASS _____

Module 8d—Theories of emotion

Description
In this module, conflicting views about how we experience emotions are explained and compared.

Outline
James-Lange theory
Cannon-Bard theory
Two-factor theory
Evolutionary theories
Review
Quiz
Recommended web links

Learning objectives
1. Compare and contrast the James-Lange and Cannon-Bard theories of emotion.
2. Explain Schachter's two-factor theory of emotion.
3. Summarize the evolutionary perspective on emotion.
4. Discuss evolutionary theorists' conclusions about the most fundamental emotions.

Guided Learning Questions
1. What did James and Lange conclude?

2. What does common sense suggest?

3. What does the James-Lange theory of emotion suggest?

Guided Learning Questions (continued)
4. What does the Cannon-Bard theory argue?

5. Finish the thought: "According to the Cannon-Bard view, people experiencing very different emotions…"

6. What was the key issue in the James-Lange vs. Cannon-Bard debate?

7. What did Schacter argue?

8. What are Schacter's two factors?

     1:

     2:

9. With respect to emotion, what did Darwin believe?

Guided Learning Questions (continued)
10. How did Darwin view emotions?

11. Which six fundamental emotions are recognized by Tomkins, Izard, and Plutchik?

    1:                           4:

    2:                           5:

    3:                           6:

12. How do evolutionary theories account for the vast number of experienced emotions?

13. Please complete the figure below:

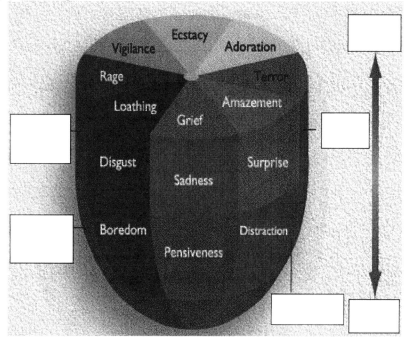

NAME _____ CLASS _____

Module 9a—Prenatal development

Description
In this module, students learn about the usual course of prenatal development.

Outline
Germinal stage
Embryonic stage
Fetal stage
Review
Quiz
Recommended web links

Learning objectives
1. Outline the major events of the germinal stage of prenatal development.
2. Outline the major events of the embryonic stage of prenatal development.
3. Outline the major events of the fetal stage of prenatal development.
4. Explain what is meant by the age of viability.

Guided Learning Questions
1. When does the prenatal period begin? When does it end?

2. Label the three stages that divide the prenatal period.

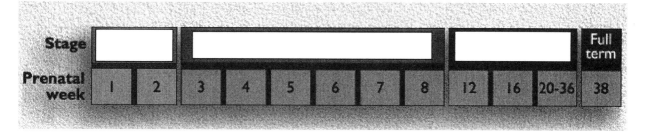

3. How long is the germinal stage?

Guided Learning Questions (continued)
4. When does the germinal stage begin?

5. Describe the process of implantation.

6. What does the placenta do?

7. Describe the seven critical events in the germinal stage.

1:

2:

3:

4:

5:

6:

7:

Guided Learning Questions (continued)

8. When does the embryonic stage begin? When does it end?

9. Why is the embryonic stage a period of great vulnerability?

10. When is the embryo's heart most vulnerable to damage?

11. When is the embryo's central nervous system most vulnerable to damage?

12. When are the embryo's eyes most vulnerable to damage?

13. When does the fetal stage begin? When does it end?

14. What is the developing organism called during this stage?

Guided Learning Questions (continued)

15. Complete the table below:

Weeks since conception	Highlights of fetal development
9	
12	
16	
20	
24	
28	
32	
36	
38	

16. When is the "age of viability" and what is it?

27. What percentage of the infants born weighing between 2lb, 13 oz. - 3lb, 4oz. survive? _____

28. Which country has the highest level of infant mortality? Which has the lowest?

NAME _____ CLASS _____

Module 9b—Erikson's theory of personality development

Description
In this module, Erik Erikson's theory about the development of personality across the life span is explained.

Outline
Childhood
Adolescence
Adulthood
Review
Quiz
Recommended web links

Learning objectives
1. Explain the nature of stage theories and the concept of psychosocial crises.
2. Describe Erikson's stages of personality development in childhood.
3. Describe Erikson's fifth stage and Marcia's work on identity.
4. Describe Erikson's stages of personality development in adulthood.

Guided Learning Questions
1. Complete the figure below:

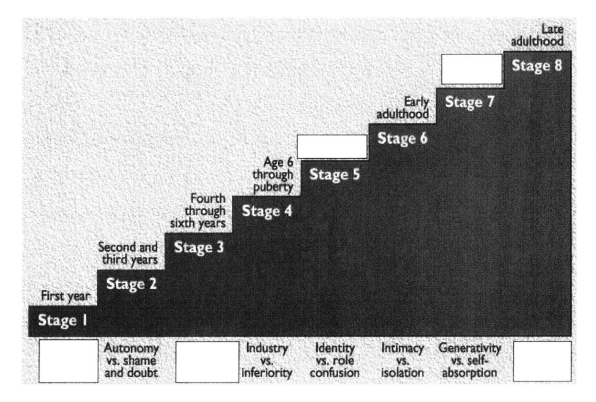

Guided Learning Questions (continued)

2. What is a psychosocial crisis?

3. Finish the thought: "According to Erikson, personality is shaped ..."

4. Please complete the table below:

Stage	Age	Crisis	Question
1			
2			
3			
4			
5			

Guided Learning Questions (continued)

5. What is an identity crisis?

6. What causes the identity crisis?

7. Please complete the table below:

Marsha's 4 types of identity status

Commitment		Crisis	
		Present	**Absent**
Present		Identity achievement	Identity foreclosure
Absent		Identity moratorium	Identity diffusion

8. Please complete the table below:

Stage	Age	Crisis	Question
6			
7			
8			

NAME _____   CLASS _____

Module 9c—Piaget's theory of cognitive development

Description
In this module, Jean Piaget's theory about the growth of children's thinking is discussed.

Outline
Sensorimotor period
Preoperational period
Concrete operational period
Formal operational period
Review
Quiz
Recommended web links

Learning objectives
1. Explain Piaget's concepts of assimilation and accommodation.
2. Describe the key characteristics of thinking during the sensorimotor period.
3. Describe the key characteristics of thinking during the preoperational period.
4. Describe the key characteristics of thinking during the concrete operational period.
5. Describe the key characteristics of thinking during the formal operational period.

Guided Learning Questions
1. What is assimilation?

2. What is accommodation?

Guided Learning Questions (continued)

3. What are Piaget's four stages of cognitive development? Complete the figure below:

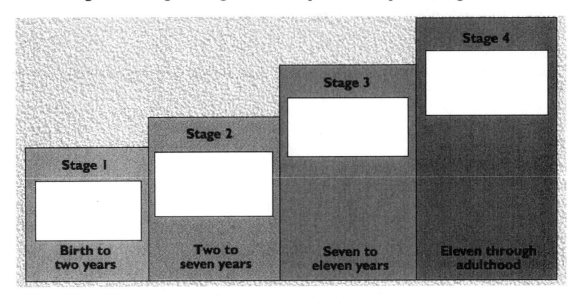

4. What are the major characteristics of the Sensorimotor period?

5. What is object permanence?

6. When do children master object permanence?

Guided Learning Questions (continued)

7. What does the mastery of object permanence indicate about children's use of symbolic thought?

8. What are the major characteristics of the Preoperational Period?

9. What is conservation?

10. When Preoperational children are shown the water beaker task, do they answer questions about volume conservation correctly? Explain.

Guided Learning Questions (continued)

11. What is centration? What is irreversibility? What role do these play for the preoperational child's performance on the water beaker task?

12. How is egocentrism characterized?

13. What happens when a preoperational child is asked to perform the 3 Mountains Task? Why?

Guided Learning Questions (continued)

14. What are the major characteristics of the Concrete Operational Period?

15. What types of conservation problems have these children mastered?

16. What are the major characteristics of the Formal Operational Period?

NAME _____   CLASS _____

Module 9d—Kohlberg's theory of moral development

Description
In this module, Lawrence Kohlberg's theory about the development of moral reasoning is covered.

Outline
Overview
Preconventional morality
Conventional morality
Postconventional morality
Review
Quiz
Recommended web links

Learning objectives
1. Describe how Kohlberg did his research on moral development.
2. Describe the key characteristics of preconventional morality.
3. Describe the key characteristics of conventional morality.
4. Describe the key characteristics of postconventional morality.

Guided Learning Questions
1. Fill-in the figure below:

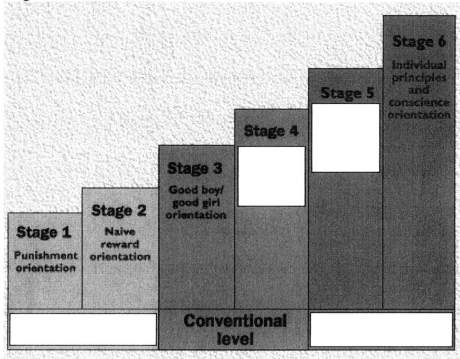

Guided Learning Questions (continued)

2. What is Level 1 in Kohlberg's model called?

3. What is the relationship between Preconventional reasoning and age?

4. What is Stage 1 characterized by?

5. What is Stage 2 characterized by?

6. Describe the Punishment orientation.

7. Describe the Naïve Reward orientation.

Guided Learning Questions (continued)

8. What is Level 2 in Kohlberg's model called?

9. What is the relationship between Conventional reasoning and age?

10. What is Stage 3 characterized by?

11. What is Stage 4 characterized by?

12. Describe the good boy/good girl orientation.

13. Describe the Authority orientation.

Guided Learning Questions (continued)

14. What is Level 3 in Kohlberg's model called?

15. What is the relationship between Postconventional reasoning and age?

16. What is Stage 5 characterized by?

17. What is Stage 6 characterized by?

18. Describe the Social Contract orientation.

19. Describe the Individual Principles & Conscience orientation.

NAME _____   CLASS _____

Module 10a—Freudian theory

Description
In this module, Sigmund Freud's influential theory of personality is explained.

Outline
Personality structure
Anxiety and defense mechanisms
Psychosexual development
Review
Quiz
Recommended web links

Learning objectives
1. List and describe the three components into which Freud divided the personality and indicate how these are distributed across three levels of awareness.
2. Explain the role of internal conflicts in Freud's theory.
3. Describe the operation of defense mechanisms.
4. Outline Freud's psychosexual stages of development and their theorized relations to adult personality.

Guided Learning Questions
1. What is psychoanalysis?

2. What does psychoanalytic theory focus on to explain personality?

3. What are Freud's three levels of awareness?

    1:

    2:

    3:

Guided Learning Questions (continued)
4. What does consciousness consist of?

5. What does preconsciousness consist of?

6. What does unconsciousness consist of?

7. Freud divided personality structure into what three components?

      1:

      2:

      3:

8. Which of these components is entirely unconscious?

9. What is the ego?

10. What guides the ego?

Guided Learning Questions (continued)

11. What is the superego?

12. What drives the superego?

13. What is the id?

14. How does the id operate?

15. According to Freud, behavior is the outcome of what?

16. What are defense mechanisms?

Guided Learning Questions (continued)

17. List and describe the seven common defense mechanisms below:

      1:

      2:

      3:

      4:

      5:

      6:

      7:

18. Freud made a startling assertion. What was it?

Guided Learning Questions (continued)

19. Please complete the diagram, below:

Psychosexual Development

Stage	Approximate Ages	Erotic Focus
[____]	0-1	[____]
Anal	[____]	Anus
Phallic	4-5	Genitals
[____]	6-12	[____]
Genital	[____]	Genitals

20. Describe the characteristics of each stage below:

Oral Stage –

Anal Stage –

Phallic Stage –

Guided Learning Questions (continued)
    Latency Stage –

    Genital Stage –

NAME _____   CLASS _____

Module 10b—Behavioral theory

Description
In this module, behavioral approaches to the understanding of personality are explored.

Outline
Structure of personality
Development of personality
Role of observational learning
Review
Quiz
Recommended web links

Learning objectives
1. Explain the behavioral view of personality structure.
2. Discuss how Skinner's principles of operant conditioning can be applied to the development of personality.
3. Discuss how Bandura's social learning theory can be applied to the development of personality.

Guided Learning Questions
1. What is Behaviorism?

2. How do Skinner's ideas differ from Freud's?

3. How did Skinner view an individual's personality?

Guided Learning Questions (continued)

4. Describe how each of the following is relevant to the development of personality:

      Negative reinforcement -

      Positive reinforcement -

      Extinction –

      Punishment -

5. Did Skinner break the development process into stages? Explain.

6. Who is Albert Bandura?

Guided Learning Questions (continued)
7. What is observational learning?

8. Finish the thought: "Bandura believes that children…"

NAME _____ CLASS _____

Module 10c—Humanistic theory

Description
In this module, students learn about humanistic approaches to the understanding of personality.

Outline
Rogers' view of personality structure
Rogers' view of personality development
Maslow's view of motivation and health
Review
Quiz
Recommended web links

Learning objectives
1. Explain the assumptions of the humanistic view.
2. Identify the single structural construct in Rogers' person-centered theory.
3. Summarize Rogers' view of personality development.
4. Explain what Maslow meant by self-actualization and summarize his findings on the characteristics of self-actualizing people.

Guided Learning Questions
1. What is Humanism?

2. What does the phenomenological approach assume?

3. What is client-centered therapy?

Guided Learning Questions (continued)

4. What is a self-concept?

5. Complete the figure below to describe two cyclical processes that promote the stability of the self-concept:

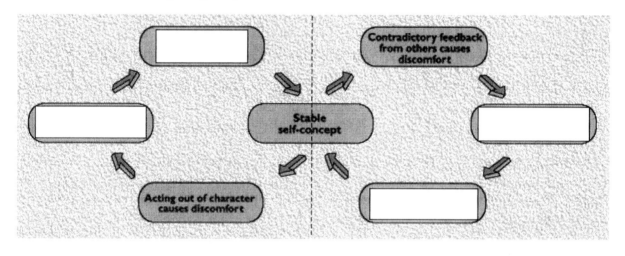

Self-Fulfilling Prophecy   **Resistance to Discordant Information**

Contradictory feedback
from others causes
discomfort

Stable
self-concept

Acting out of character
causes discomfort

6. What is incongruence?

7. According to Rogers, what kind of parenting fosters congruence? Incongruence?

8. What does incongruence lead to?

Guided Learning Questions (continued)
9. Please complete the figure of Maslow's Needs Hierarchy below:

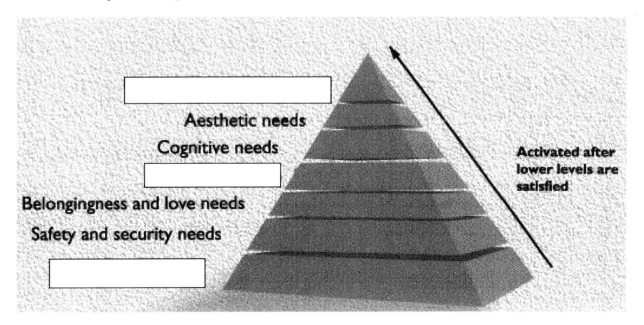

Aesthetic needs

Cognitive needs

Belongingness and love needs

Safety and security needs

Activated after lower levels are satisfied

10. What are growth needs?

11. What are the characteristics of self-actualizing people?

NAME _____   CLASS _____

Module 10d—Biological theory

Description
In this module, students learn about biological perspectives on personality.

Outline
Sheldon's theory
Eysenck's theory
Behavioral genetics research
Review
Quiz
Recommended web links

Learning objectives
1. Describe Sheldon's three body types and their hypothesized links to personality.
2. Summarize Eysenck's view of the structure of personality.
3. Summarize Eysenck's view of the development of personality.
4. Describe recent behavioral genetics research on the heritability of personality.

Guided Learning Questions
1. What body types did Sheldon identify? Describe each.

      1:

      2:

      3:

2. What traits did Sheldon associate with each body type?

Guided Learning Questions (continued)

3. How does Eysenck view personality structure?

4. According to Eysenck, what role does genetic influence play in conditioning?

5. According to Eysenck, why are some people introverted?

6. Do identical twins show more similar personality attributes than fraternal twins do? Explain.

Guided Learning Questions (continued)

7. What do the results of the Minnesota study suggest about the role of genetic influence in personality?

8. Do the results support the claim that personality is largely inherited? Explain.

NAME _____   CLASS _____

Module 11a—Anxiety disorders

Description
In this module, the symptoms and causes of four types of anxiety disorders are reviewed.

Outline
Types of anxiety disorders
Biological causal factors
Environmental causal factors
Review
Quiz
Recommended web links

Learning objectives
1. Describe four types of anxiety disorders and discuss their prevalence.
2. Discuss genetic and neurochemical contributions to the etiology of anxiety disorders.
3. Discuss the contributions of conditioning and cognitive factors to the etiology of anxiety disorders.

Guided Learning Questions
1. What are anxiety disorders?

2. How common are anxiety disorders?

3. What are the four principle types of anxiety disorders? Complete the figure below:

Guided Learning Questions (continued)
4. What are the symptoms of Generalized Anxiety disorder?

5. What are the symptoms of a phobic disorder?

6. What are the three most common phobias?

      1:

      2:

      3:

7. What are the symptoms of a panic disorder?

8. What is agoraphobia?

Guided Learning Questions (continued)

9. What are the symptoms of an obsessive-compulsive disorder?

10. What are compulsions?

11. What does a concordance rate indicate?

12. What does the concordance rate indicate about the role of genetic influence in the development of anxiety disorders?

13. How does Valium work?

14. How do the drug-therapies for obsessive-compulsive disorder work?

Guided Learning Questions (continued)

15. How does classical conditioning play a role in the development of phobias?

16. How does operant conditioning contribute to the maintenance of anxious responses?

17. According to cognitive theorists, what are the characteristics of anxious thought? Complete the figure below:_____

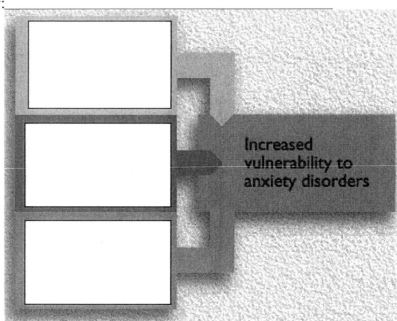

Increased vulnerability to anxiety disorders

18. How did you interpret the word "growth" in the sentence, "The doctor examined little Emma's growth."

Guided Learning Questions (continued)

19. According to the cognitive view, why are some people prone to anxiety disorders?

20. Can stress precipitate the onset of an anxiety disorder? Explain.

NAME _____   CLASS _____

Module 11b—Mood disorders

Description
In this module, the symptoms and causes of severe mood disorders are explained.

Outline
Types of mood disorders
Biological factors in mood disorders
Environmental factors in mood disorders
Review
Quiz
Recommended web links

Learning objectives
1. Describe the two major mood disorders and discuss their prevalence.
2. Explain how genetic and neurochemical factors may be related to the development of mood disorders.
3. Explain how cognitive factors (patterns of attribution) may be related to the development of mood disorders.
4. Explain how interpersonal factors and stress may be related to the development of mood disorders.

Guided Learning Questions
1. What are mood disorders?

2. What are the two basic types of mood disorders?

      1:

      2:

3. How would you characterize unipolar mood disorder?

Guided Learning Questions (continued)

4. How would you characterize bipolar mood disorder?

5. How common are mood disorders? Which type of mood disorder is more common?

6. When is the onset of bipolar disorder most likely? Is the onset of depressive disorders related to age?

7. Describe the emotional symptoms of depression.

Guided Learning Questions (continued)

8. Describe the cognitive symptoms of depression.

9. Describe the behavioral symptoms of depression.

10. Describe the emotional symptoms of manic episodes.

Guided Learning Questions (continued)

11. Describe the cognitive symptoms of manic episodes.

12. Describe the behavioral symptoms of manic episodes.

13. Does heredity create a predisposition to mood disorders? Explain.

14. How do traditional antidepressants work?

Guided Learning Questions (continued)
15. How do newer antidepressants (such as Prozac) work?

16. What are attributions?

17. Attributions can be analyzed along three dimensions. What are they?

    1:

    2:

    3:

18. Please complete the figure below:

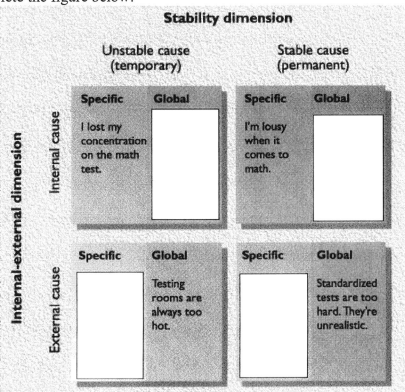

Guided Learning Questions (continued)

19. According to the learned helplessness model, which attributional style is most likely to lead to a sense of helplessness and depression?

20. What are the effects of rumination (reflection) on depression?

21. According to behavioral approaches, what leads to depression?

22. How does stress precipitate mood disorders?

NAME _____ CLASS _____

Module 11c—Schizophrenic disorders

Description
In this module, students learn about the symptoms and causes of schizophrenic disorders.

Outline
Symptoms and subtypes
Biological factors in schizophrenic disorders
Environmental factors in schizophrenic disorders
Review
Quiz
Recommended web links
Simulation – Clinical Diagnosis

Learning objectives
1. Describe the general characteristics (symptoms) of schizophrenia and its prevalence.
2. Describe four schizophrenic subtypes.
3. Explain how genetic vulnerability, neurochemical factors, and structural abnormalities in the brain may contribute to the etiology of schizophrenia.
4. Summarize evidence on how family dynamics and stress may be related to the development of schizophrenia.

Guided Learning Questions
1. What do schizophrenic disorders involve?

2. How common are schizophrenic disorders?

3. What is the central feature of schizophrenic disorders?

Guided Learning Questions (continued)

4. What are other symptoms of schizophrenia?

5. What are the four types of schizophrenia?

       1:

       2:

       3:

       4:

6. What are the characteristics of paranoid schizophrenia?

7. What are the characteristics of catatonic schizophrenia?

8. What are the characteristics of disorganized schizophrenia?

Guided Learning Questions (continued)

9. What are the characteristics of undifferentiated schizophrenia?

10. Based on the results of twin studies, do genetics influence the development of schizophrenia?

11. How do medications for schizophrenia work?

12. How do the ventricles of non-schizophrenics differ from those of people afflicted with schizophrenia?

13. How does communication deviance contribute to the development of schizophrenia?

14. What is expressed emotion?

Guided Learning Questions (continued)

15. How does expressed emotion affect the likelihood of relapse?

16. Please complete the figure below:

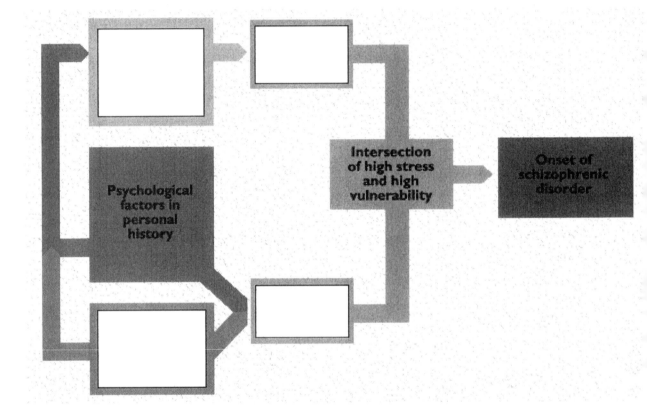

NAME _____   CLASS _____

Module 11d—Insight therapies

Description
In this module, students learn about insight therapy as an approach to the treatment of psychological disorders.

Outline
Overview
Psychoanalysis
Client-centered therapy
Review
Quiz
Recommended web links

Learning objectives
1. Identify the three major categories of therapy.
2. Explain Freud's view of the roots of neurotic disorders.
3. Explain the logic of psychoanalysis and describe the techniques by which analysts probe the unconscious.
4. Discuss resistance and transference in psychoanalysis.
5. Identify the elements of therapeutic climate in Rogers' client-centered therapy.
6. Discuss the therapeutic process in client-centered therapy.

Guided Learning Questions
1. What is the professional treatment of psychological disorders and problems called?

2. What are the three broad categories of approaches to treatment?

      1:

      2:

      3:

3. What are the characteristics of insight therapies?

Guided Learning Questions (continued)

4. What are neuroses?

5. According to Freud, what causes neurotic problems?

6. What is the logic underlying psychoanalysis?

7. How does free association contribute to psychoanalysis?

8. How does dream analysis contribute to psychoanalysis?

9. How does resistance contribute to psychoanalysis?

Guided Learning Questions (continued)
10. How does transference contribute to psychoanalysis?

11. What are psychodynamic therapies?

12. According to Rogers, what causes most personal distress?

13. How do client-centered therapies try to help clients?

14. According to Rogers, what are the 3 requirements for a supportive therapeutic climate?

     1:

     2:

     3:

15. What is the therapist's role in client-centered therapy?

NAME _____ CLASS _____

Module 11e—Behavioral and biomedical therapies

Description
In this module, students learn about behavioral and biomedical approaches to the treatment of psychological disorders.

Outline
Behavioral therapies
Biomedical therapies
Review
Quiz
Recommended web links

Learning objectives
1. Describe the goals and procedures of systematic desensitization.
2. Describe the goals and procedures of aversion therapy.
3. Describe the principal categories of drugs used in the treatment of psychological disorders.
4. Discuss the biochemical bases of drug treatments for psychological disorders.

Guided Learning Questions
1. What is the professional treatment of psychological disorders and problems called?

2. What are the three broad categories of approaches to treatment?

1:

2:

3:

3. What are behavioral therapies based on?

4. What do Behavioral therapists use to change overt behaviors?

Guided Learning Questions (continued)

5. What is the original behavioral therapy?

6. What is the goal of systematic desensitization?

7. What three steps make up systematic desensitization?

      1:

      2:

      3:

4. According to Wolpe, how does systematic desensitization work?

5. What is aversion therapy?

Guided Learning Questions (continued)

6. How does aversion therapy work?

7. What are biomedical therapies?

8. Drug treatments for psychological disorders fall into three major groups. What are they?

      1:

      2:

      3:

9. What do antianxiety drugs do?

10. What are some examples of antianxiety drugs?

11. How do antianxiety drugs work?

Guided Learning Questions (continued)

12. What are the two most common side-effects of antianxiety drugs?

13. What do antipsychotic drugs do?

14. What are some examples of antipsychotic drugs?

15. How do antipsychotic drugs work?

16. What is Tardive Dyskineasia?

17. What do antidepressants do?

Guided Learning Questions (continued)
18. What are some examples of antidepressant drugs?

19. How do antidepressant drugs work?

20. What are the two principle classes of antidepressant drugs?

    1:

    2:

21. How do these drugs work?

22. What do selective seratonin reuptake inhibitors do?

NAME _____   CLASS _____

Module 11f—Types of stress

Description
In this module, students learn about the nature of stress and the various types of stress.

Outline
Frustration
Conflict
Change
Pressure
Review
Quiz
Recommended web links

Learning objectives
1. Define and describe stress.
2. List the four principal types of stress.
3. Describe how frustration contributes to stress.
4. List and define the three types of conflict.
5. Describe the SSRS and its three qualifications.
6. Define the two types of pressure.

Guided learning Questions
1. What is stress?

2. What are the four principal types of stress?

    1:

    2:

    3:

    4:

Guided Learning Questions (continued)

3. When does frustration occur?

4. When does conflict occur?

5. List and describe the three types of conflict.

      1:

      2:

      3:

6. What does the Social Readjustment Scale measure?

Guided Learning Questions (continued)

7. Finish the thought: "Thousands of studies have shown that….."

8. What are the three qualifications to the conclusion above?

     1:

     2:

     3:

9. What does pressure involve?

10. What are the two types of pressure discussed?

     1:

     2:

Guided Learning Questions (continued)

11. Which shows a stronger correlation with psychological symptoms, the SRRS or pressure? Explain.

NAME _____   CLASS _____

Module 11g—Responding to stress

Description
In this module, students learn about responses to stressful life events.

Outline
Emotional responses
Physiological responses
Behavioral responses
Review
Quiz
Recommended web links

Learning objectives
1. List the three types of responses to stress.
2. List emotions triggered by stress.
3. Describe the relationship between physiological arousal and performance.
4. Describe the three stages of the General Adaptation Syndrome.
5. Describe the two major pathways that the brain uses to send signals to the endocrine system in response to stress.
6. List and describe maladaptive coping strategies.
7. List and describe adaptive coping responses.

Guided learning Questions
1. The subjective perception of threat typically leads to responses at several levels. What are the three levels discussed?

     1:

     2:

     3:

Guided Learning Questions (continued)

2. What feelings are often elicited by stress?

3. What is the *inverted-U hypothesis*?

4. What is the optimal arousal level for moderately-difficult tasks? For simpler tasks? For more complicated tasks?

Guided Learning Questions (continued)
5. What did Hans Selye do?

6. Based on the general adaptation syndrome, what are the three stages of stress responses? What happens in each stage?

      1:

      2:

      3:

7. When stressed, what are the two major pathways the brain uses to send signals to the endocrine system?

      1:

      2:

Guided Learning Questions (continued)

8. List the common maladaptive coping strategies.

9. What is catastrophic thinking?

10. What are three types of strategies involved in constructive coping? Provide an example of each.

       1:

       2:

       3:

NAME _____ CLASS _____

Module 12a—Attribution processes

Description
In this module, students learn how attributional thinking plays a key role in our social lives.

Outline
Internal versus external attributions
Kelley's model
Weiner's model
Attributional biases
Review
Quiz
Recommended web links

Learning objectives
1. Explain what attributions are and describe the distinction between internal and external attributions.
2. Summarize Kelley's theory of attribution.
3. Summarize Weiner's theory of attribution.
4. Describe some types of attributional bias.

Guided Learning Questions
1. What are attributions?

2. Where do internal attributions locate the causes of events?

3. To what do internal attributions ascribe events?

Guided Learning Questions (continued)
4. Where do external attributions locate the causes of events?

5. To what do external attributions ascribe events?

6. According to Kelley's covariation model, when people attempt to infer the causes of an actor's behavior, they consider three factors. What are they?

     1:

     2:

     3:

7. Describe the following:

     Consensus -

     Consistency -

     Distinctiveness -

Guided Learning Questions (continued)
8. What kind of attribution does low consistency favor?

9. When is high consistency compatible with an internal attribution?

10. When is high consistency compatible with an external attribution?

11. What did Bernard Weiner conclude?

12. Please complete the figure below:

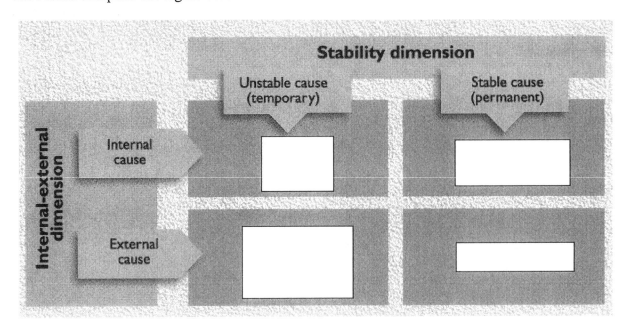

13. What kind of attribution fosters feelings of depression?

14. Finish the thought: "Studies of attributional bias show that the actor's view of his behavior ..."

15. What do observers tend to do?

16. What is the fundamental attribution error?

Guided Learning Questions (continued)

17. What do actors tend to do?

18. What is the self-serving bias? How do people tend to explain failures? Successes?

NAME _____ CLASS _____

Module 12b—Theories of love

Description
In this module, a variety of theoretical perspectives on the nature and experience of love are explored.

Outline
Passionate versus companionate love
Sternberg's triangular theory
Lee's styles of loving
Love as attachment
Review
Quiz
Recommended web links

Learning objectives
1. Explain the distinction between passionate and companionate love.
2. Describe Sternberg's triangular theory of love.
3. Describe Lee's six styles of loving.
4. Summarize the evidence on love as a form of attachment.

Guided Learning Questions
1. What is passionate love?

2. What is companionate love?

3. According to Sternberg, companionate love can be subdivided into what?

     1:

     2:

Guided Learning Questions (continued)

4. What is intimacy?

5. What is commitment?

6. Complete the figure below:

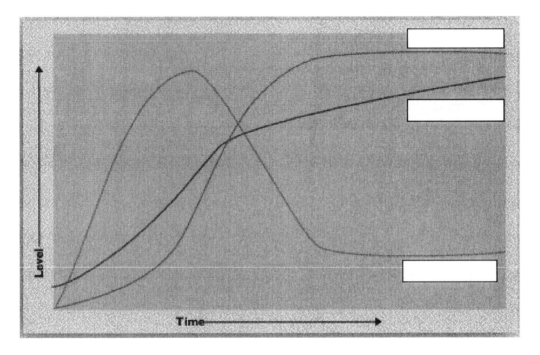

7. How does passion change with time?

8. How does intimacy change with time?

Guided Learning Questions (continued)

9. How does commitment change with time?

10. Complete the figure below:

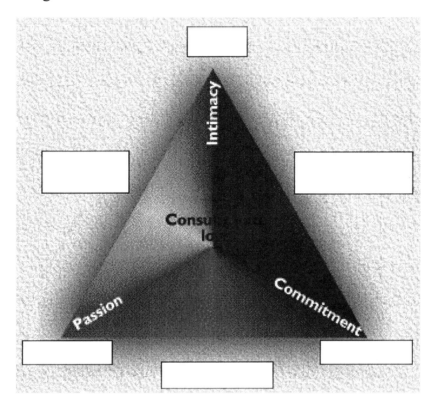

11. Describe the following:

Liking -

Romantic love -

Infatuation –

Guided Learning Questions (continued)

Fatuous love -

Empty love -

Companionate love -

Consummate love -

12. What did John Alan Lee argue?

13. Describe the following:

LUDUS -

MANIA -

PRAGMA –

EROS -

Guided Learning Questions (continued)
    AGAPE -

    STORGE -

14. What is attachment?

15. Please complete the figure below:

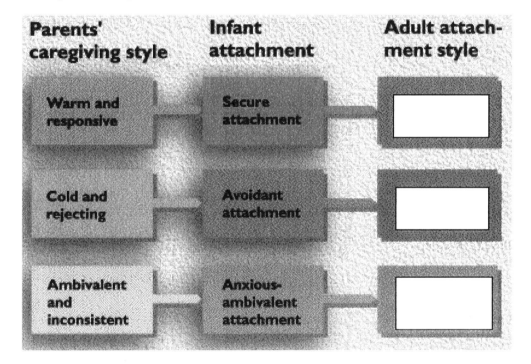

16. Describe secure adults. What percentage of people studies were secure adults?

17. Describe avoidant adults. What percentage of people studies were avoidant adults?

18. Describe anxious-ambivalent adults. What percentage of people studies were anxious-ambivalent adults?

NAME _____   CLASS _____

Module 12c—Attitude change

Description
In this module, students learn about the diverse theories that have been proposed to explain the mechanisms at work in attitude change.

Outline
Learning theory
Balance theory
Dissonance theory
Self-perception theory
Elaboration likelihood model
Review
Quiz
Recommended web links
Simulation – Social Judgment

Learning objectives
1. Discuss how learning processes can contribute to determining attitudes.
2. Explain how Heider's balance theory can account for attitude change.
3. Explain how cognitive dissonance can account for the effects of counter attitudinal behavior.
4. Relate self-perception theory to attitude change.
5. Explain the two routes to persuasion in the elaboration likelihood model.

Guided Learning Questions
1. How do advertisers try to take advantage of classical conditioning?

2. Explain how operant conditioning can play a role in attitude change.

Guided Learning Questions (continued)

3. Explain how observational learning can play a role in attitude change.

4. What is Fritz Heider's Balance Theory based on?

5. Describe Heider's idea of a balanced relationship.

6. Describe Heider's idea of an imbalanced relationship.

7. According to Heider, what does imbalance create?

Guided Learning Questions (continued)

8. Describe three problems with Heider's Balance Theory

       1:

       2:

       3:

9. What does Leon Festinger's Dissonance Theory assume?

10. Finish the thought: "According to Festinger, when related cognitions (beliefs) contradict each other …"

11. What does this tension do?

12. In Festinger and Carlsmith's experiment, which group rated the dull task as more enjoyable? What did Festinger and Carlsmith conclude?

Guided Learning Questions (continued)

13. What had Daryl Bem argued?

14. What does conventional wisdom assume?

15. What has Bem suggested?

16. What is Bem's alternative explanation of Festinger and Carlsmith's results?

17. What is the Elaboration Likelihood model?

18. Describe the Central Route.

Guided Learning Questions (continued)
19. Describe the Peripheral Route.

20. According to the Elaboration Likelihood model, which route creates more durable attitude changes? Why?

NAME _____   CLASS _____

Module 12d—Prejudice

Description
In this module, students learn about some of the social processes that foster prejudice.

Outline
Prejudice versus discrimination
Stereotypes
Attributional bias
Learning factors
In-groups versus out-groups
Review
Quiz
Recommended web links

Learning objectives
1. Distinguish between prejudice and discrimination.
2. Relate stereotypes and attributional bias to prejudice.
3. Explain how observational learning and operant conditioning can contribute to prejudice.
4. Relate the concepts of in-groups and out-groups to prejudice.

Guided Learning Questions
1. What is prejudice?

2. Like other attitudes, prejudice includes three elements. Describe each.

     1:

     2:

     3:

Guided Learning Questions (continued)
3. What is discrimination?

4. Finish the thought: "Perhaps no factor plays a larger role in prejudice than …"

5. What are stereotypes?

6. What are the most common stereotypes in our society based on?

7. What do stereotypes tend to involve?

8. Why do stereotypes persist?

9. How often was the shove coeds labeled as "violent behavior" when the actor was white? When the actor was black?

Guided Learning Questions (continued)

10. Are men and women generally credited for successes equally? Explain.

11. What is the fundamental attribution error?

12. What do defensive attributions involve?

13. Describe the role of observational learning in the development of prejudice attitudes.

14. Describe the role of operant conditioning in the development of prejudice attitudes.

15. Do people tend to evaluate in-group and out-group members differently? Explain.

16. Finish the thought: "The illusion of homogeneity in the out-group …"

NAME _____ CLASS _____

Simulation 1—Experimenting with the Stroop test

Description
In this simulation, students are led through a specific experiment where they will serve as the subjects, asking them to apply what they have learned about the experimental method. They inductively figure out the hypothesis, the independent and dependent variables, the experimental and control conditions, and so on. Then they run the experiment, using the Stroop task. After running the experiment, students analyze their data, graph their results, and work through their implications. The net result is that students see the experimental method in action in ways that should greatly increase their understanding of the intricacies of experimentation. Students can print out their results or email them to an instructor.

Outline
Learn about the Stroop test and experimentation
Do the Stroop experiment
Look at your data again after you have done the experiment

Guided Learning Questions
1. J.R. Stroop compared subjects' performance on 3 related tasks. Describe each task below:

    Task 1 –

    Task 2 –

    Task 3 –

2. What are hypotheses?

3. Which of the hypotheses given did you prefer? Why?

Guided Learning Questions (continued)

4. What is an independent variable?

5. What is the independent variable in this experiment?

6. What is a dependent variable?

7. Which of the choices is the best dependent variable for this experiment?

8. What is an experimental group?

9. What is a control group?

10. Which task represents the experimental condition in this experiment?

Guided Learning Questions (continued)
11. Do the experiment and fill in your data below:

	Control Condition (color patches)	Experimental Condition (word in incongruent colors)
1		
2		
3		
4		
5		
6		
7		
8		
9		
10		

12. What is the mean for the Control Condition? What is the SD for the Control Condition?

13. What is the mean for the Experimental Condition? What is the SD for the Experimental Condition?

Guided Learning Questions (continued)

14. Please graph your results below (show all numbers and details):

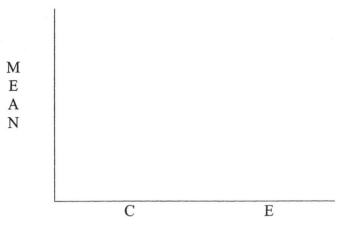

C = control condition
E = experimental condition

15. What is the value of your t test? Is your t test significant? What is the p value (e.g., $p < .05$)?

16. Did your data support your chosen hypothesis? Explain.

17. Which hypothesis has previous research supported?

NAME _____   CLASS _____

Simulation 2—Hemispheric specialization

Description

In this simulation, students get a taste of how research on cerebral specialization is conducted, as they serve as subjects in a perceptual asymmetry study. Spatial stimuli (pictures of hands) are flashed onscreen very briefly in students' left or right visual field. They are asked to indicate whether the pictures show a left hand or a right hand. After completing 24 trials, students can calculate the mean recognition time for the left versus the right visual field and check the statistical significance of their results. Because perceptual asymmetry effects tend to be rather weak and unreliable, we then lead the students through a "debriefing" in which they consider a variety of reasons why they may or may not have obtained the expected results. This portion of the simulation should increase students' sophistication about the experimental method. Students can print out their results or email them to an instructor.

Outline

Learn about this demonstration
Adjust the display time
Do the demonstration

Guided Learning Questions

1. Finish the thought: "Previous research has shown that stimuli requiring visuo-spatial processing are typically recognized more quickly by ..."

2. What is the independent variable in this experiment?

3. What is the dependent variable in this experiment?

Guided Learning Questions (continued)

4. What is our hypothesis for this experiment?

5. Do the experiment and fill in your data below:

	Left Visual Field	Right Visual Field
1		
2		
3		
4		
5		
6		
7		
8		
9		
10		
11		
12		

6. What is the mean for the Left Visual Field Condition? What is the SD for the Left Visual Field Condition?

Guided Learning Questions (continued)
7. What is the mean for the Right Visual Field Condition? What is the SD for the Right Visual
Field Condition?

8. Please graph your results below (show all numbers and details):

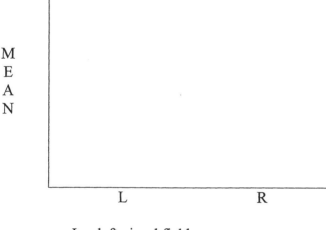

L = left visual field
R= right visual field

9. What is the value of your t test? Is your t test significant? What is the *p* value (e.g., *p* < .05)?

10. Do your data support the hypothesis? Explain.

Guided Learning Questions (continued)

10A. If your data do NOT support the hypothesis, then answer the questions below. If the data do support the hypothesis, then skip to B below.

List 2 of the 5 possible reasons given why the hypothesis was not supported.

1:

2:

Now, list the remedy for each of these below:

1:

2:

10B. If your data DO support the hypothesis, then answer the questions below. If the data do support the hypothesis, then skip these questions.

List the artifacts mentioned that could have tainted the results of the experiment.

1:

2:

Now, list the remedy for each of these below:

1:

2:

NAME _____   CLASS _____

Simulation 3—The Poggendorff illusion

Description
In this simulation, students get to play with the Poggendorff illusion to see what factors influence its effects. For each presentation of the illusion, students try to line up the slanted line on the right with the slanted line on the left. After each trial, they get immediate feedback about how close they came. Across the series of 10 trials, the width of the box, the angle of the slanted lines, and so forth are manipulated. After the trials are completed, the students get to see their data in a graphical format. The data have implications about which factors make the illusion most powerful. Students can print out their results or email them to an instructor.

Outline
Learn about this demonstration
Do the demonstration

Guided Learning Questions
After reading the introduction and completing the experiment, complete the graphs below (show all numbers and details):

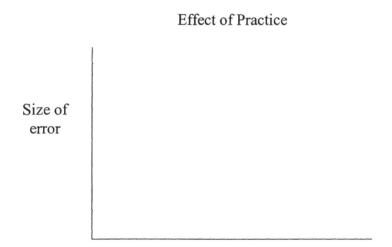

Effect of Practice

Size of
error

1. Do the data show a practice effect? Explain.

Guided Learning Questions (continued)

Effect of Angle

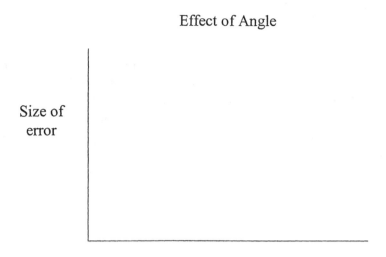

Size of
error

2. Do the data show an effect of angle? Explain.

Effect of Width

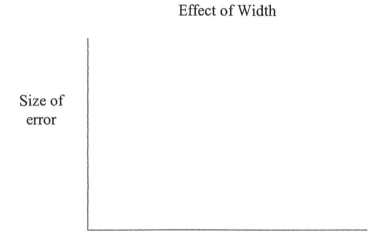

Size of
error

3. Do the data show an effect of width? Explain.

Guided Learning Questions (continued)

Effect of Line Through Top

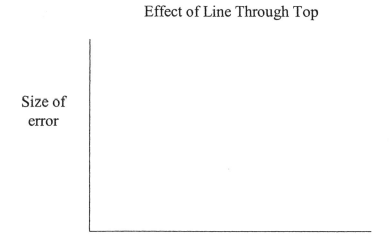

Size of
error

4. Do the data show an effect of line placement? Explain.

NAME _____   CLASS _____

Simulation 4—Shaping in operant conditioning

Description
In this simulation, students get to see shaping in action as they attempt to shape Morphy the virtual rat to press a lever 15 times. The simulated reinforcement consists of electrical stimulation delivered to pleasure centers in Morphy's brain, so we don't have to introduce complications such as allowing time for Morphy to eat a food reward. Throughout the shaping process, students can click on a CHECK TRAINING button to see the response hierarchies that Morphy has acquired for various locations in the experimental apparatus. It takes about 10-15 minutes to shape Morphy to criterion. The exercise gives students a good feel for how shaping works. After shaping Morphy to press the lever 15 times, students can choose to shape Morphy to make a variety of other responses. Students can print out their results or email them to an instructor.

Outline
Learn about shaping Morphy to press the lever
Train Morphy to press the lever
Learn about shaping Morphy to make another response
Train Morphy to make another response

Guided Learning Questions
1. What is a Skinner box?

2. What does shaping involve?

Guided Learning Questions (continued)

3. How long did it take you to shape Morphy to press the leaver 15 times?

4. How many reinforcements did you deliver?

5. Shape Morphy to perform a new behavior. You choose what the new behavior is. What new behavior did you pick? How did you shape the behavior (e.g., I started by reinforcing any movement to the center, then I only reinforced movement to the front center square, then I...).

NAME _____ CLASS _____

Simulation 5—Memory processes I

Description
In this simulation, students serve as subjects in a brief experiment that introduces them to several memory phenomena. The experiment is modeled after Craik and Lockhart's (1972) research on levels of processing. Students are shown a series of 36 words and asked questions about them that are intended to produce structural, phonemic, or semantic encoding. After processing all 36 words, students are given a free recall measure and a recognition measure of their retention of the 36 words. After comparing their retention on these two measures, the program plots their retention based on the words' placement in the list, to see if a serial position effect occurred. Finally, the program plots their retention as a function of the level of processing engaged. Students can print out their results or email them to an instructor.

Outline
Learn about this demonstration
Do the demonstration

Guided Learning Questions
1. Finish the thought: "Recall measures of retention require….."

2. Finish the thought: "Recognition measures of retention require….."

3. Do the two different measures of retention represent independent variables or dependent variables?

4. Which measure of retention yields a higher estimate of retention? Why do you think that is?

Guided Learning Questions (continued)

5. After completing the experiment, graph your data below (show all numbers and details):

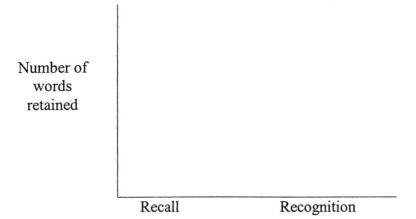

6. When does the serial position effect occur?

7. When does the primacy effect occur?

8. When does the recency effect occur?

Guided Learning Questions (continued)
9. Graph your data below (show all numbers and details):

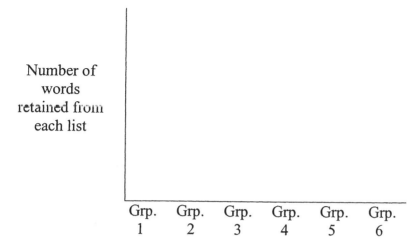

Number of
words
retained from
each list

Grp.   Grp.   Grp.   Grp.   Grp.   Grp.
1   2   3   4   5   6

10. What does the levels-of-processing theory propose?

11. What does structural encoding emphasize?

12. What does phonemic encoding emphasize?

13. What does semantic encoding emphasize?

Guided Learning Questions (continued)

14. Which type of encoding do you think produces the deepest processing? Were you right? Explain.

15. Do the three different types of encoding represent independent variables or dependent variables?

16. Graph your data below (show all numbers and details):

Seconds

Structural   Phonemic   Semantic

Type of Encoding

17. "Deeper levels of processing require more time." Do your data support this claim? Explain.

Guided Learning Questions (continued)
18. Graph your data below (show all numbers and details):

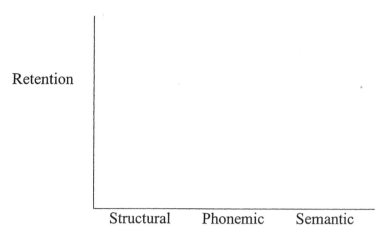

19. "Deeper levels of processing result in better retention." Do your data support this claim? Explain.

NAME _____ CLASS _____

Simulation 6—Memory processes II

Description

In this simulation, students see twelve lists of ten words. After each list, students are given a recall test. After all twelve lists are presented, students take a recognition test and indicate the confidence of their recognition judgments. The items on each list are categorically related (e.g., things that have to do with music), but the categorical exemplar (e.g., music) is not included. Typically, students will incorrectly recall and recognize, with a high degree of confidence, the categorical exemplars (e.g., music) as presented items. The activity also asks students to identify the independent and dependent variables, and allows students to print or send their results by email.

Outline

Learn about this demonstration

Take part in the study

Guided Learning Questions

| Please note: This experiment is longer than the others |

1. Do the free recall and recognition measures of your memory represent independent variables or dependent variables?

2. How many of the twelve nonpresented target words did you freely recall?

3. What percentage of the time did you incorrectly report that nonpresented target words had been stimulus words?

Guided Learning Questions (continued)

4. To what do Roediger and McDermitt (1995) attribute the prevalence of false memories uncovered in this research paradigm?

      1:

      2:

NAME _____   CLASS _____

Simulation 7—Problem solving

Description
In this simulation, students work on a classic problem that has been used extensively in research on problem solving. They participate in a fun, challenging test of their problem solving skills and gain some insight into how psychologists study problem solving. Our version of the problem is called the Hobbits and Orcs problem. Three hobbits and three orcs need to get across a river in a small boat, but you can't let the orcs outnumber the hobbits on either side of the river, or the orcs will eat the hobbits. Students try to solve the problem onscreen by sending various combinations of hobbits and orcs across the river. Students who get frustrated can ask the program to show them a solution. Students who solve the problem can go on to a more complex version involving five hobbits and five orcs. Along the way, students get feedback about certain aspects of their problem-solving style. Students can print out their results or email them to an instructor.

Outline
Learn about the Hobbits and Orcs problem
Try solving the problem with three hobbits and three orcs
Try solving the problem with five hobbits and five orcs

Guided Learning Questions
1. Solve the problem (the solution is available if you don't solve the problem on the first try). How many tries did it take you to solve the problem?

2. How long did it take you (on average) to think of your first move? What is typical for students working on this problem?

3. Solve the more advanced problem (the solution is available if you don't solve the problem on the first try). How many tries did it take you to solve the problem?

Guided Learning Questions (continued)

4. Finish the thought: "Research suggests that people who are strong planners..."

NAME _____   CLASS _____

Simulation 8—Psychological testing: Measuring your creativity

Description
In this simulation, students take a genuine psychological test designed to assess their creativity. The test is the Remote Associates Test developed by Mednick and Mednick (1967). Although the test was a popular commercial scale for many years, it is now out of print, and the authors graciously allowed us to use the test for our educational purposes. Students self-administer the 30-item scale onscreen. After they complete the test, the program walks them through information on the scale's norms, standardization, reliability, and validity. Thus, we use the process of taking an interesting test as a vehicle to acquaint students with a variety of crucial concepts in psychological testing. Students can print out their results or email them to an instructor.

Outline
Learn about this demonstration
See the instructions and practice items
Take the test

Guided Learning Questions
1. What is the first step in the development of a psychological test?

2. According to the Mednick's view, what is the key to creative thinking?

3. Why are test norms needed?

Guided Learning Questions (continued)
4. What does a percentile score indicate?

5. What is the percentile score for a male with a raw score of 15 on the RAT? What does this mean?

6. What is reliability?

7. What is validity?

8. What is construct validity?

9. Scores on the RAT are negatively correlated with scores on conformity and authoritarian measures. Explain how this supports the idea that the RAT is a valid measure of creativity.

NAME _____   CLASS _____

Simulation 9—Clinical Diagnosis

Description
In this simulation, students try to distinguish various psychological disorders from each other (undifferentiated schizophrenia, major depression, and obsessive-compulsive disorder). Students view videotaped interviews with three people, identify each person's symptoms, and render tentative diagnoses. Students can print out their results or email them to an instructor.

This activity is designed to provide students with an opportunity to apply what they've learned. It is not designed to provide extensive background information about psychological disorders. Students should be familiar with the symptoms of schizophrenia, major depression, bipolar disorder, and obsessive-compulsive disorder *before* they do this activity.

Guided Learning Questions
1. Watch the video-taped interviews with Barbara. What are her symptoms?

2. What is Barbara's diagnosis (be as specific as possible)?

Guided Learning Questions (continued)

3. Watch the video-taped interviews with Chuck. What are his symptoms?

4. What is Chuck's diagnosis (be as specific as possible)?

5. Watch the video-taped interviews with Etta. What are her symptoms?

What is Etta's diagnosis (be as specific as possible)?

When you have completed the diagnoses, you can use the SIMULATION SUMMARY option to print, email, or copy (by hand) all of your performance information.

NAME _____ CLASS _____

Simulation 10—Social Judgment

Description
In this simulation, students make personality judgments about the people they see in pictures (ten men and ten women). The simulation helps students identify the independent and dependent variables that were used, and identify the difference between experimental and control conditions. The activity concludes by helping students to see if their results support the proposed hypothesis. Students can easily calculate descriptive statistics for their personality judgments, graph their results, perform t-tests for each personality judgment, and see an overview of their results. Students can print out their results or email them to an instructor.

Outline
Learn about this demonstration
Do the demonstration

Guided Learning Questions
1. What did Karen Dion, Ellen Berscheid, and Elaine Walster demonstrate?

2. What is the independent variable in this study?

3. What is the dependent variable in this study?

4. What is an experimental group?

Guided Learning Questions (continued)

5. What is a control group?

6. Which task represents the experimental condition?

7. Which two traits are typically unaffected?

8. Pick one of the traits that you evaluated. List the scores that you gave for each trait.

Trait name _____

	Experimental Condition	Control Condition
1		
2		
3		
4		
5		
6		
7		
8		
9		
10		

Guided Learning Questions (continued)

9. What is the mean for the Control Condition? What is the SD for the Control Condition?

10. What is the mean for the Experimental Condition? What is the SD for the Experimental Condition?

11. Please graph your results below (show all numbers and details):

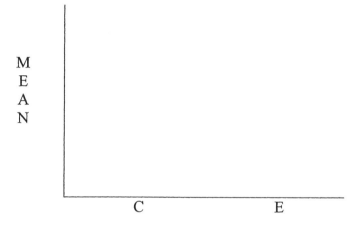

M
E
A
N

         C   E

C = control condition
E = experimental condition

12. What is the value of your t test? Is your t test significant? Do your data support the hypothesis? Explain.

An overview showing all of your results is available at the end of the simulation.

8 CREDITS AND REFERENCES

The Credits component of *Psyk.trek* provides required lists of permissions for the reproduction of photos, illustrations, and videos, along with editorial, production, and contributor credits, as well as the usual legalese about licensing, and so forth. You access the Credits from *Psyk.trek's* opening screen by clicking the picture of the infant on the visual cliff that hangs in the sky on the left. The opening screen of the Credits section provides a list of the various types of information available (see ❶ in Figure 8.1). You can go directly to a particular part of the Credits section by clicking an entry in this list. The red buttons in the lower right corner are used for navigation. The red backward button ❷ moves you back one screen. Inside the Credits, the red up button ❸ returns you to the opening screen of the Credits component. If you are at the opening screen of the Credits, the up button takes you back to *Psyk.trek's* opening screen and the navigation cube. The red forward button ❹ moves you forward one screen.

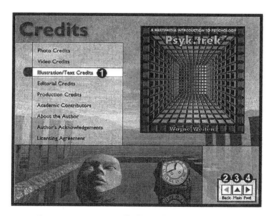

Figure 8.1. The opening screen of the Credits component in *Psyk.trek*.

REFERENCES

Baker, W., Hale, T., & Gifford, B. R. (1997). Technology in the classroom: From theory to practice. *Educom Review, September/October,* 42-50.

Craik. F. I. M., & Lockhart, R. S. (1972). Levels of processing: A framework for memory research. *Journal of Verbal Learning and Verbal Behavior, 11,* 671-684.

Forsyth, D. R., & Archer, C. R. (1997). Technologically assisted instruction and student mastery, motivation, and matriculation. *Teaching of Psychology, 24,* 207-212.

Mathie, V. A., in collaboration with Beins, B., Benjamin, L., Ewing, M., Iijema Hall, C., Henderson, B., McAdam, D., & Smith, R. (1993). Promoting active learning in psychology courses. In T. V. McGovern (Ed.), *Handbook for enhancing undergraduate education in psychology.* Washington, DC: American Psychological Association.

Mednick, S. A., & Mednick, M. T. (1967). *Remote Associates Test Examiner's Manual.* Boston: Houghton Mifflin.

Paivio, A. (1986). *Mental representations: A dual coding approach.* New York: Oxford University Press.

Stalling, R. B., & Wasden, R. E. (1998). *Study guide for Weiten's Psychology: Themes & Variations.* Pacific Grove, CA: Brooks/Cole.

Weiten, W. (1998). *Psychology: Themes & Variations.* Pacific Grove, CA: Brooks/Cole.